MARLON BRANDO

MARLON BRANDO

Pyramid Illustrated History of the Movies

by
René Jordan

General Editor: **TED SENNETT**

PYRAMID
PUBLICATIONS
NEW YORK

MARLON BRANDO
Pyramid Illustrated History of the Movies

ISBN 0-515-03128-3

Library of Congress Catalog Card Number: 73-78305

Published by Pyramid Publications, a division of Pyramid Communications, Inc. Its trademarks, consisting of the word "Pyramid" and the portrayal of a pyramid, are registered in the United States Patent Office.

PYRAMID COMMUNICATIONS, INC.
919 Third Avenue, New York, New York 10022

(graphic design by anthony basile)

FOR JOHN

PREFACE

By TED SENNETT

"The movies!" Flickering lights in the darkness that stirred our imaginations and haunted our dreams. All of us cherish memories of "going to the movies" to gasp at feats of derring-do, to roar with laughter at clownish antics, to weep at acts of noble sacrifice. For many filmgoers, the events on the screen were not only larger than life but also more mysterious, more fascinating, and—when times were bad—more rewarding. And if audiences could be blamed for preferring movies to life, they never seemed to notice, or care.

Of course the movies have always been more than a source of wish-fulfillment or a repository for nostalgic memories. From the first unsteady images to today's most experimental efforts, motion pictures have mirrored America's social history, and over the decades they have developed into an internationally esteemed art.

As social history, movies reflect our changing tastes, styles, and ideas. To our amusement, they show us how we looked and behaved: flappers with bobbed hair and bee-stung lips cavorting at "wild" parties; gangsters and G-men in striped suits and wide-brimmed hats exchanging gunfire in city streets; pompadoured "swing-shift" Susies and dashing servicemen, "working for Uncle Sam." To our chagrin, they show us the innocent (and sometimes not so innocent) lies we believed: that love triumphs over all adversity and even comes to broad-shouldered lady executives; that war is an heroic and virtually bloodless activity; that fame and success can be achieved indiscriminately by chorus girls, scientists, football players, and artists. To our edification, they show us how we felt about marriage in the twenties,

7

crime in the thirties, war in the forties, big business in the fifties, and youth in the sixties. (Presumably future film-goers will know how we felt about sex in the seventies.)

As an influential art, motion pictures are being studied and analyzed as never before by young filmgoers who are excited by the medium's past accomplishments and its even greater potential for the future. The rich body of films from *Intolerance* to *The Godfather*; the work of directors from Griffith to Kubrick; the uses of film for documenting events, ideas, and even emotions—these are the abundant materials from which film courses and film societies are being created across the country.

PYRAMID ILLUSTRATED HISTORY OF THE MOVIES also draws on these materials, encompassing in a series of publications all the people, the trends, and the concepts that have contributed to motion pictures as nostalgia, as social history, and as art. The books in the series range as widely as the camera-eye can take us, from the distant past when artists with a vision of film's possibilities shaped a new form of expression, to the immediate future, when the medium may well undergo changes as innovative as the first primitive movements.

PYRAMID ILLUSTRATED HISTORY OF THE MOVIES is a tribute to achievement: to the charismatic stars who linger in all our memories, and to the gifted people behind the cameras: the directors, the producers, the writers, the editors, the cameramen. It is also a salute to everyone who loves movies, forgives their failures, and acknowledges their shortcomings, who attends Bogart and Marx Brothers revivals and Ingmar Bergman retrospectives and festivals of forthcoming American and European films.

"The movies!" The cameras turn and the flickering images begin. And again we settle back to watch the screen, hoping to see a dream made real, an idea made palpable, or a promise fulfilled. On that unquenchable hope alone, the movies will endure.

ACKNOWLEDGMENTS

I wish to thank Patrick Veitch and Adolfo Rizo for help during research; and Stephen Reichl of Paramount, Ralph Alexander of Avco Embassy, Alex Black of Universal, and Films Incorporated for their cooperation in letting me see the Brando films. I should also like to specially thank Jerry Vermilye for the photographs.

CONTENTS

MARLON BRANDO

n August 1950, during the pre-
iere engagement of *The Men* at
ew York's Radio City Music Hall,
Iarlon Brando first scowled from
te huge screen at a stunned movie
idience. He slurred his speech
id stretched his silences in an
:stasy of noncommunication. He
y low, like a sated tiger, ready to
ounce again at the slightest
unger pain. There was something
iimal, primal, atavistic in him,
id everyone responded—in iden-
fication, revulsion, or alarm. Out
' such fears and longings stars are
:eated and myths are born.
rando was both, from the very
rst close-up.

He became the substance of end-
·ss dreams, the escape valve for
iyriad repressions. His style was
innibalized and badly digested by
ountless imitators, but far more
nportant, it spilled into everyday
fe. He permeated America and
:eped abroad through a movie
eve. The world at large became
is gallery of mirrors.

The Brando image dies hard and
irvives in every boy—or even
irl—who feigns indifference to
ide alienation, risks spiritual frost-
ite to keep his cool, and erases
very distinction of age, class or
ven gender by indiscriminately
alling everyone "man." Beats,
Iippies, Yippies, cats: the record
hanges but they are all still in
·rando's groove, even though their

CHAPTER I

A MYTH IS BORN

acquaintance with the wild, early
Brando may go no further than the
Late Late Show.

Yet however blurry the Xerox
copies may be getting, Brando was
the original. He was the first
Method actor to become a movie
star. Girls were swooning over his
sullen masculinity while he was
being proclaimed "the world's
greatest performer." Attempting to
define the phenomenon, a Hollywood wag lamented: "I'm afraid we
have a genius for a matinee idol."
Brando was neither, but he was
strong enough to survive being
called "the Valentino of the bop
generation," "the walking hormone
factory," and "the male Garbo."

Beyond all the name-calling, he
was "the Method actor," and the
tag proved a blessing and a curse.
In a consumer society Brando
became a standard brand. With a
label, he could be identified
instantly on the cluttered Hollywood shelves, to be discarded by
obsolescence as soon as the fashion
waned. But his magic lingered on,
and two decades and 27 movies
later, one wonders what his
method was—or if it ever was
really *the* Method.

In the late Forties a new form of

theatrical expression began taking roots in America. Basically, the so-called Method was an adaptation of Constantin Stanislavsky's teachings to an entirely different national temperament. The brooding intro-spection Stanislavsky expounded in the Moscow Art Theatre was ideal for that Slavic self-absorption that boils into frenzy in Dostoyevsky's novels or simmers into gentle defeat in a Chekhovian cherry orchard.

America was too vital and ener-getic for all that. The country had barely recovered from a Depres-sion followed by war and then by guilt-ridden affluence. There was a dynamism in the air, an aggres-siveness inimical to the passive acceptance of fate. In late-forties America the Stanislavsky system changed gears and pushed boldly forward, driven by teachers like Stella Adler and Lee Strasberg. And in Marlon Brando's sturdy frame it found the perfect instru-ment for its tormented athleticism: the pantomime of living the night-mare aspects of the American dream.

No actor in films—except Oli-vier at his best—has used his body with such cunning sense of revela-tion in reflex. Brando's restless hands, for example, have shouted a thousand and one unspoken words. They fumbled with the zipper of his leather jacket each time The Wild One was challenged to aban-don his childish identification b costume. The wrists rose and fell surrendering to grief, as he silentl mourned his slaughtered pigeon in On the Waterfront. Those rest less fingers are still stroking the electrically charged fur of a ca while The Godfather reviews, with imperial boredom, the petty crimi nal business on the daily agenda.

With Brando, a highly special ized form of acting came to the movies. Maximilian Schell, who acted with him in The Young Lions astutely pinpoints it when he says "He discovered early that in these times an actor cannot say 'I love you' but has to cover his feeling with a gesture." Thus, Brando' acting is a way of telegraphing emo tion through motion. It is easy to see why he quickly abandoned the theater—a realm of words—for the movies, where the intimacy o the camera could change his teleg raphy into sheer telepathy, mutat ing Morse into Mesmer through hypnotic close-ups of his all revealing eyes.

Millions loved him for all the wrong reasons, and from the start he was caught in the dilemma of the serious actor who becomes an immensely popular star. By the most general of definitions, every actor is a character actor in the sense that he must play a character other than himself. Brando wanted o go further, widening his territory as he expanded or contracted his personality by assuming others. His Hollywood saga can be chronicled as a fight to be an actor in the full sense of the word, while the commercial standards of producers and audiences demand that their favorites be "personalities."

In Brando the struggle was intensifed by his novelty as a screen performer. Twenty years after the emergence of sound, movie acting had not fully recovered from its impact. Even the most body-oriented of performers — such as Gable and Cagney —were occasionally forced to indulge in verbal binges imposed by the screenplay. Brando subverted all this with his alleged "mumbles." He had the intuition to recognize that people are mostly inarticulate and that to present them realistically an actor has to fumble a few of his words. Like accomplished jugglers, actors with perfect elocution invoke awe, but Brando lets his words fall where they may, and the audience is galvanized into instant identification.

Yet Brando never slurs a line that is intrinsic to the meaning of the character, and when the text warrants it, as in *Julius Caesar*, he enunciates with unfailing pitch and clarity. He has always known how to concentrate on the basic; his mumbles are really asides his characters speak to themselves. They are as expressive as the movements of his hands; the only difference is that they are audible, *vocal gestures*. When a Brando film is dubbed into another language, his lines are verbalized by actors following a script and attempting lip synchronization. The effect is fascinating and disturbing, for the deciphered mumbling becomes worthless repetition, unilluminating verbiage. Only Brando had been able to make lines mean something when they were really nothing.

It is said that Brando can imitate anyone after watching him for ten minutes, and he used this mimetic power to observe people at large, sense their reality and refine it dramatically. It is not true that Brando invented a type: he merely formalized the vague mannerisms of an alienated generation. He had his finger on the pulse of a feverish world and diagnosed the complaint as acute rebellion.

Still, there was something ambivalent in the way he rebelled. He was brutal-tender, offensive-defensive, menacing-vulnerable. Even at his most ferocious, as in *The Wild One*, there was an undercurrent of conformity, a longing to be accepted and loved. Time and again the Brando characters repent, often after being cruelly beaten. When Brando went beyond stardom into movie mythology, it was as a two-faced Janus—half-good, half-bad—and, most significant of all, essentially redeemable.

In *The Wild One* his rebel image has undeniable components of the thirties movie gangsters, with glimpses of the kingly surliness of Edward G. Robinson in *Little Caesar* or the restless, dancing-on-the-spot tension of James Cagney in *The Public Enemy*. But these men channeled their rejection of the ruling order into crime, while Brando's characters stopped short of it. Brando's unsocial behavior could be discarded at will; he was appealing to a youthful audience because he was adopting an attitude, passing through a phase, enormously enjoying a masquerade, but never making a life style out of it. Cagney and Robinson had no way back on the road to damnation, but Brando offered rebellion with a return stub.

This discardable quality makes big stars. Girls, for instance, could become platinum Harlows with peroxide and good will, or crimson Clara Bow vamps with a bottle of henna, or Monroe-like nymphs courtesy of Clairol. When time took its toll of them, the disguises could be discarded before they turned into housewives and mothers. The Brando façade was also seductively transitory: a fear of age

is endemic in a civilization geared to the cult of youth, and he was a safe idol to be imitated and then left behind, consigned with boots and leather jacket to the back of the closet.

For Brando the wild image was also a passing phase, but when he tried to move out of it, he found himself trapped. He was the cherished fantasy of many, and they wouldn't let him go. He began to be chided for playing himself, for having a very limited bag of tricks, for doing all that was condoned in other players. As a high priest of the Method, he was asked to sink his soul into his roles, with no emerging identification marks.

Brando paid for all the popular misconceptions about Method acting. Stanislavskian teachers know that no actor should *become* the character: that would be transitory schizophrenia and therefore inapplicable as art. What a good Method actor does is to play himself within the role, using his instrument—body, voice, mind—in the presentation of a different human being. The daring of Brando's career is that he let so many souls inhabit him, from an Okinawan peasant to Bonaparte, from Marc Antony to an aging Sicilian *mafioso*. One of the constant pleasures of watching his films is to see Brando play himself in others, with unlimited variety.

He dared to experiment and was berated for his brave failures by the same critics who applauded others for playing it safe. People become emotional when they discuss Brando: more than any other actor he evokes love-hate reactions. For those who grew up with him, his rebellions are a reminder of their own betrayed ideals. "What a waste of talent" is the standard line when highbrows refer to him. The line changes to "What a pretentious bore" as soon as the brows get lower.

The Actors Studio background is perennially held against him. Brando was the White Hope of a group of highly talented performers, and when he decided to work in films he was the equivalent of a class valedictorian in philosophy who decides to make a fortune in the stock market. If Brando had been another type of artist, he could have hibernated in a garret, painting or sculpting away until he achieved immortality through death. Film is the most communal of arts, and he had to work within a system, always fighting it and even subverting it. Yet his passing into movies is forever lamented by the theatrical intelligentsia, as if a commercialized and moribund Broadway theatre had anything better to offer.

No other actor has ever gone in roller-coaster fashion from such pinnacles of praise to such abysses of vituperation. By turns reviled and revered, rejected and resurrected, Brando has been declared finished with monotonous regularity. Like a phoenix too frequent, he has risen from the ashes of his incandescent talent to prove time and again that he is still with us, the most resourceful, inventive, daring, annoying, contradictory, and brilliant actor in America.

Bud was his nickname, and even in the early photographs of a chubby, tousle-haired, well-scrubbed little boy there is the shadow of a scowl around the flinty eyes, the hint of a dissatisfied pout around the lips. The tiny round face just won't open; it is tightly shut somewhere below the cheekbones, like a brooding cherub's with a touch of mischief.

Method actors draw on their past to whip up the emotions they recreate. That much about the Actors Studio secret rites was known by audiences in Brando's highly publicized early days in Hollywood. The audience and sometimes the critics wondered what gloomy pictures Brando was dredging up in his mind as he went through his angry outbursts, the murderous rages that shook the screen. Magazine profiles of Brando in the fifties abound in quests for his final essence and often read like starry-eyed versions of the search for Rosebud in *Citizen Kane*.

Secretive to the point of obsession, Brando made sure his private world was never explored. He not only shunned self-revelation but deliberately obscured the facts. In his first *Playbill* biography he said he was born in Bangkok, the son of a zoological explorer. In further capsule biographies for theatrical programs the father's profession

CHAPTER II
BUDDING INTO BRANDO

changed and so did the birthplace, to include Mindanao, Rangoon, and Bombay.

This tendency to enshroud himself in mystery has intensified with the years. Interviews with Marlon Brando read like sardonic put-ons in which he seems to enjoy confounding reporters by answering each question with another. Collating them, the facts seldom match; the inner feelings, never.

In fact, the young man who claimed to be a zoologist's son from Bangkok was born in Omaha, Nebraska, on April 3, 1924, to a manufacturer of chemical feed products and pesticides. Marlon Brando—a star name if there ever was one—was really his father's name, derived from French ancestors who spelled it Brandeau. Brando, Sr., has been described by his daughters as a frustrated actor. His wife, Dorothy Pennebaker, was an amateur actress, always involved in little-theater activities wherever the family moved during Buddy's childhood. Her son was only two when she appeared at the local Omaha Playhouse, co-starring in O'Neill's *Beyond the Horizon* with another aspiring Nebraskan, Henry Fonda.

Called "Do" by everyone, Mrs. Brando instilled a love of beautiful pretense in her children. Frances and Jocelyn became, respectively, an artist and an actress. When Buddy was six, the family moved to Evanston, Illinois, and then to nearby Libertyville. Charming Do Brando was the center of home activities; Brando later claimed his father was aloof and uninterested. In Libertyville High School Buddy played football and was on the track squad. He wanted to be a sports star, the better to impress Brando, Sr., but according to one of his teachers he always had to stay after classes to atone for a prank, missing practice too often to achieve any distinction in the field.

When he turned fifteen, his father gave him a set of Afro-Cuban drums and—in a houseful of aspiring artists—Buddy found a new source of attention by keeping the neighbors awake while beating on the bongos. The message of the tom-toms was received by his parents. It was time to clamp some discipline on the youth, so he was sent to Shattuck Military Academy in Faribault, Minnesota. To this day, Brando calls it "the Military Asylum."

In Shattuck he took part in theatricals, and in his first two stage appearances he played a corpse strung on the gallows and an explorer in an Egyptian tomb. The

mild thrill of amateur acting soon palled, and he was again playing his favorite part: the uncontrollable rebel.

He hated a life regimented by clocks, so he buried a bell clapper that turned out to be irreplaceable in wartime; no bell chimed in Shattuck until years after VE Day. He became adept at hair-tonic pranks: once he sprinkled an obscenity on a wall and then set fire to it, in a blaze of challenging profanity. Then he put firecrackers in a teacher's bedroom, sprayed a trail of Vitalis down the corridor, and set fire to it. The charred hair tonic made a telltale beeline to his own bedroom door, and Cadet Brando managed to get himself expelled in 1943, shortly before graduation.

Back home in Libertyville, he announced his intention to enter the clergy. His parents argued him out of it but not out of the puritanical streak that stayed with him through the years. He then volunteered for the Army and was turned down because of a trick knee, acquired in his desultory football days. Almost as a punishment he took a grueling job as a tile fitter for a drainage construction firm. He deeply hated it but kept at it for six weeks before quitting.

Buddy zigzagged between a desire to stay home and a compulsion to leave as soon as possible. Brando hinted at the reasons when he made painful revelations to Truman Capote, who incorporated them in a *New Yorker* profile entitled "The Duke in his Domain." Dorothy Brando was a Midwestern Bovary, a woman of potential brilliance shackled to the drudgery of being a housewife. When her theatrical illusions withered away, she found an escape in drink. There were days, Brando told Capote, when his mother would disappear until local bars called the house saying: "We've got a lady down here. You'd better come get her."

Frances and Jocelyn had already moved to New York, and Brando, Sr., agreed to send Buddy away also. In the summer of 1943 he arrived, shortly after his nineteenth birthday, to stay with his married sister Frances in a Manhattan apartment. His aim was to study theater and perhaps to fulfill Do Brando's dreams of conquering Broadway.

In the fall he entered the Dramatic Workshop at the New School for Social Research. Erwin Piscator, the director of the project, soon detected in Brando "an inner rhythm that never fails." The boy began to attract attention in Dramatic Workshop productions and received his first good notice when *The Morning Telegraph* signaled his performance in Hauptmann's *Hannele's Way to Heaven*, in which he played the schoolteacher and

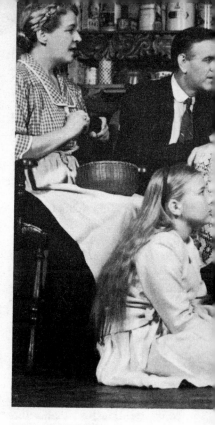

then the angel in the play's dream sequence.

His school work included appearances in adaptations of two Molière plays and in Shakespeare's *Twelfth Night*. By the summer of 1944 he was part of a stock company directed by Piscator in Sayville, Long Island. He made his first professional appearance on Broadway in *Bobino*, a children's play by Stanley Kauffmann, as "a giraffe and a guard." According to the author, "his role consisted of

being hit on the head and falling down, but he managed a way of falling that, without being obtrusive, was individual."

In his student years Brando supported himself with fly-by-night jobs such as running an elevator in Best and Company's department store—and quitting because saying "lingerie" out loud embarrassed him. The bashful, intense young man impressed two of the most important people in his early formation. Elia Kazan recognized his talent and supervised his first directing job in a student production of *Hedda Gabler*. And in Stella Adler, Brando found the dedicated teacher who goaded him out of his shyness. She sensed the electricity in the young man and led him into creating what Brando called "lightning states" on stage.

At twenty he had his first association with a Broadway hit when he played fifteen-year-old Nels, the son in John van Druten's dramatization of Kathryn Forbes' *I*

Remember Mama. But even then he had a reputation as a highly idiosyncratic actor. When he answered a casting call for *O Mistress Mine,* an Alfred Lunt-Lynn Fontanne vehicle by Terence Rattigan, he was given a script and coldly told to read from it. He looked at the pages, unable to summon any feeling. When they asked him to speak up and say something, he clearly enunciated "Hickory, dickory, dock" and walked out.

He did not return to Broadway until 1946. Harold Clurman was casting Maxwell Anderson's *Truckline Café,* and Stella Adler asked him to give her star pupil a chance. Clurman had seen Brando in *I Remember Mama* and wondered how this dutiful boy in a family play could turn into a veteran who murders his unfaithful wife. Elia Kazan was the producer, and he underscored Adler's recommendation, so Clurman gave Brando a try.

First rehearsals were disastrous. Brando was completely withdrawn and introspective, barely lifting his eyes from the floor, mumbling lines in a whisper that was inaudible beyond the third row. Mulling over the final decision before firing him, Clurman gave Brando a last chance. He dismissed the cast for a long lunch hour and, left alone with the blocked apprentice, forced him to speak his lines louder and louder, until Brando was screamin[g] like a madman. Seizing on th[e] actor's frenzy, Clurman made hi[m] climb a rope up to the rafters an[d] down, still yelling at the top of hi[s] lungs.

On opening night, February 7[,] 1946, Brando evoked the sam[e] fury. The impulse lasted throug[h] every one of the few performance[s] of the play's short run. He brough[t] audiences to their feet, wo[n] repeated ovations and began to b[e] reckoned an upcoming star.

Guthrie McClintic then cas[t] Brando opposite Katharine Corne[ll] in Bernard Shaw's *Candida.* Cor[-] nell found him "a beautiful March[-] banks," but reviewers were les[s] kind: Stanley Kauffmann wrote tha[t] despite some touching moment[s] his poet "talked like a cab drive[r] and moved like a third baseman.["] He stayed with the show for a whil[e] and then gave up his $300 a wee[k] salary for $30 a week to help [a] cause he believed in: in Ber[n] Hecht's *A Flag is Born* he playe[d] David, a Jewish refugee involve[d] in the struggle to found the new state of Israel.

Late in 1946 he was chosen a[s] Tallulah Bankhead's leading man i[n] Jean Cocteau's *The Eagle Has Two Heads.* The play is the kind o[f] dreamlike allegory French classica[l] acting is perfect for; it was late[r] made into a static, oddly riveting film with Edwige Feuillère and

Jean Marais. Brando was hopelessly ill-equipped for the part of the revolutionary who invades a queen's boudoir with murderous intentions but ends up falling in love with her.

The script had Bankhead greeting him with an ominous line: "You are my death." It turned out to be almost prophetic because Brando's stage antics brought the actress close to apoplexy. In the first act she had a 22-minute monologue throughout which Brando was supposed to stand transfixed by the flowing cadences of Cocteau's prose. He could not sustain the rapt concentration this pageant demanded and began sampling the props, fingering his costume.

Things got even worse during Bankhead's death scene. The revolutionary shot the queen, and Bankhead did a marvelous descent, head first, down a flight of courtly steps. As she was hanging perilously and uncomfortably, the repentant murderer was required to drink a frothy cup of poison. After being upstaged all night by Cocteau and Bankhead, Brando demanded equal time. His death scene took several minutes as he staggered about the stage, leaving no table unturned, no sofa intact. The audience went into a delighted uproar. Needless to say, Bankhead demanded his ejection, and he was replaced by Helmut Dantine during the Boston tryout.

The experience turned Brando away from a Broadway theater focused on the star system. He studied and traveled in Europe and returned to New York in mid-1947, to be drawn by the magnetism of *A Streetcar Named Desire*, a Tennessee Williams play everyone was calling a masterpiece before it had even reached rehearsal stage.

Elia Kazan was the director, Irene Selznick the producer. He favored Brando for the part of Stanley Kowalski, but she was holding out for John Garfield. When Garfield did not materialize, Selznick was willing to gamble on Brando but sought the approval of the author. Brando was broke and hitchhiked to Provincetown where Williams was vacationing. A storm had knocked out the electricity, and Brando arrived as an aspiring performer only to end up a handyman. He went into the cellar, tinkered with the fuses, and turned on the lights. Then he read for Kowalski and illuminated the part into a blaze. Williams agreed he was the best choice for the role.

Rehearsals began on October 1, 1947, and were again problematical. Brando sat next to his co-star Kim Hunter and fretted: "They should have got John Garfield for Stanley. He was right for the part, not me." Little by little Brando began edging into the character:

A STREETCAR NAMED DESIRE (1947).
In his stage role of Stanley Kowalski.

he mumbled speech pattern, the slouching body, the defensive arrogance. Better than any other director, Kazan knew how to work with him; he let him improvise and take his time, not imposing the mood from outside but letting it grow from within.

On the night of December 4, 1947, Kowalski was born of a piece. Reviews were excellent and the audience reaction electric. Brando was not satisfied and regarded Kowalski as an unfinished creation. He played the role for a year and a half, keeping it fresh with a different attack every night. Remembering the long run, Kim Hunter has said that, for example, in the scene where he went through Blanche's trunkful of worthless possessions, Brando would shift emphasis and concentrate on different objects every time. He would force Hunter to play Stella as motherly one night and impatient the next. "He has such an uncanny sense of the truth," Hunter recalls, "that he yanks you into his own sense of reality." Brando was perfecting what later on, in films, would evolve into his player's trick to hold the winning cards in each scene.

He became the conductor and rode a different *Streetcar* every night, liberally changing his pace, his movements, even his lines. Producer Selznick once had Tennessee Williams revisit the play so

that he would persuade Brando to follow the text. Williams was enchanted with what he saw and told Selznick: "Let him play it that way, it's better." Ceaselessly he would experiment, and once he deliberately went on half drunk on beer—just as Stanley usually was—to get deeper into the man's marrow. Brando's performance as Kowalski is considered a landmark in the American theater, but many years later he was still complaining: "He was not complete. I think I missed his gaiety."

After a year's run, Brando was bored with repetitions and had taken to boxing and sparring with the stagehands during intermissions, to keep his energy going. He accidentally took a punch that broke his nose but insisted on playing the third act. He then went to the hospital where his nose was set. Irene Selznick wanted him back in the show as soon as possible, so next morning she arrived to check on his condition.

Hearing she was on her way, Brando took off all the bandages, dabbed his face with iodine and terrified his lady producer when she saw him turned into a bloody mess. Between moans Brando promised he would come back to the theater in two days, but she begged him to stay in the hospital as long as it was necessary. Brando got himself a two-week rest period, but his tampering with the bandages had after-effects: his nose was not properly set and remained forever crooked. When Irene Selznick finally learned of his deception and its aftermath, she attributed his screen success to this accident. "Before it, he was just too beautiful," she said.

His hit in *Streetcar* did not alter the bohemian, devil-may-care pattern of his life. Wally Cox, who had gone through the fourth grade with Brando in Evanston, had long forgiven Buddy for once tying him to a fence pole for half a night when they were children. Cox was a bright young comedian when they both shared an apartment someone called "the Mecca of confusion." Stories about the place are plentiful: at one time a door-to-door salesman peeked in and fled, shouting, "You don't need a vacuum cleaner—you need a plow". Shelley Winters remembers that Brando and Cox once decided to paint the living room, got as far as doing one wall, and then, for a whole year, the pails of paint and the caked brushes lay there, while visitors gingerly stepped around them.

The confusion stopped when it was time to work. By 1948 Elia Kazan, Robert Whitehead and Cheryl Crawford founded the Actors Studio that eventually came under Lee Strasberg's control. The senior group was formed by nucleus of actors who were destined to become top rank: Mauree Stapleton, Eli Wallach, Anne Jackson, Montgomery Clift, Patrici Neal, David Wayne, Tom Ewel Mildred Dunnock, Karl Malden and Kevin McCarthy were amon them. Brando's roles in worksho productions were a constant sourc of admiration to fellow members He seemed to have no limits an was astounding as a Hapsbur prince in *Reunion in Vienna* in th afternoon, then ran to get an ova tion as Kowalski.

Sometime during these years Brando's past caught up with him His mother and father came t New York to see him open i *Streetcar,* and cocky, rebelliou Brando surprised everyone b revealing what a loving, deferentia son he was. Dorothy Brando late came to New York for an extende visit, and at his mother's feet h placed all the glittering triumph she had longed for. It made no dif ference. Far gone into drink, sh insulted her son, threw things a him, and slowly turned his pity int hatred.

In "The Duke in his Domain," Brando told Capote about how hard he had tried to save hi mother from alcoholism until he became indifferent. "My love was not enough," he said, "and I let her fall, because I couldn't take it any more—watch her breaking apart in front of me." This traumatic experience has haunted him all his life, and in the spring of 1972, in an interview printed by the Italian magazine *Oggi*, he told Roger Houze about his mother's descent into alcoholism which turned "a sensitive, intelligent lady into a mean, hard, insufferable woman." I adored her and she disappointed me in a damnable way," he told Houze. "That's why I make women suffer. They give me a feeling of taking revenge on my mother. I have tried to act normally but I have not succeeded."

This bitterness would not set in until the late fifties, when Brando entered into stormy marriages and relationships only Strindberg could describe properly. Early in 1950 he was young, hopeful, and very ambitious. He wanted to conquer new media and did his one television play, *Come Out Fighting*, for NBC. This was also the year when he was lured by Stanley Kramer's offer of $40,000 for his first picture, *The Men*.

"I don't have the moral strength to say no to that kind of money," he declared, but also insisted that his move was temporary. He would occasionally do one or two pictures, but "his future and his life" was in the theater. He said farewell to Broadway, not knowing it would turn out to be a long goodbye. A headline jokingly proclaimed him "Marlon of the Movies." For better or worse, that is exactly what he would turn out to be.

From the moment he arrived in Hollywood Brando declared holy war on the cities of the plain, from Culver to Burbank. Refusing to socialize, he shut himself in Birmingham Veterans Hospital in Van Nuys and spent four weeks in a ward with the paraplegics, picking up clues for the character of the paralyzed soldier he was to play in *The Men*.

He moved in a wheelchair and went everywhere with his ward mates. Once, in an all-night diner, they were approached by a revivalist who claimed that faith would make them walk. Brando listened to her spiel and touched her Bible, and she fainted as he got up, screaming: "I can walk." On another occasion he was taken by taxi to producer Stanley Kramer's office but arrived so late that he ran from the cab, forgot his folded wheelchair and almost gave the driver a heart attack. He was having childlike fun while preparing seriously for the part, a work system many directors later misunderstood as lack of discipline.

For *The Men* Brando wanted a change of pace, but after a few days of trying to pry him away from Kowalski, director Fred Zinnemann gave up. Kenneth Williams had been the hero's name in the screenplay, but he was hastily rebaptized Wilocek. The Polish-American name was relooped into

THE WILD YEARS

the earlier takes, and for stronger personal identification he was nicknamed Bud, just like the adolescent Brando. Yet another pattern was set by making him an orphan; in his 27 films up to 1973 Brando has never had a visible father or mother on the screen.

He didn't need them, for Bud Wilocek emerged by spontaneous generation in the first shot, as he lies paralyzed, his brow contorted with agony as his off-screen voice leavens despair with sarcasm in his initial words: "That's funny, very funny. I was afraid I was going to die. Now I'm afraid I'm going to live." Brando—the body-conscious actor of magnetic sex-appeal— paradoxically started his film career as a paralyzed, impotent man who rages against his fate, reluctantly marries his girlfriend, and faces an uncertain future with a valiant shrug.

The part proved ideally suited for Brando's movie debut. If *A Streetcar Named Desire* had been his first film, the highly theatrical shock of a larger-than-life performance might have been more than 1950 audiences were ready for. He was served to the public piecemeal and had to play the part at half-nast; the forced immobility and sexlessness were appealing to women, who found him a disquietingly attractive but tragically manageable male. For men, an element of competition was eliminated: Brando could be pitied and his arrogance forgiven as a form of desperate bravado. He was an actor before he ever stood in front of a camera, but *The Men* provided the balanced ingredients to make him a star.

Bud Wilocek was the first—and purest—example of the Freudian man-child, the neurotic fifties'

THE MEN (1950). As Ken.

Everyman Brando would bring to the movies. He battles with the father image, portrayed as a tough doctor by Everett Sloane; he is uncertain about his physical control down to the level of possible bed-wetting; he is wary of women, especially after a well-calculated subplot involving a tart who fleeces his buddy (Jack Webb). With Teresa Wright, the persistent girl who loves him, he is at his most savage; when she first stands by his hospital bed, he shouts at her viciously: "Don't look at me, you stupid idiot," but the way he hides his face in his folded arms belies the cruelty, revealing an ill-concealed yearning for protection.

In *The Men* Brando has the freshness of the novice, plus an insecurity that operates like a brake. In several scenes, one can almost feel the actor asking himself: "Am I going too far?" The part absorbs all the hesitancy and makes Wilocek all the more likable for it, but under the broken body and the childish tantrums there is a vein of iron, a suggestion of a toppled god, a maimed Apollo.

Fred Zinnemann, a director whose tact and discretion are often misinterpreted as academicism or blankness, saves *The Men* from sinking into self-pitying pathos, despite the heavy-handed Kramer production, the neat manipulations of Carl Foreman's script, and the

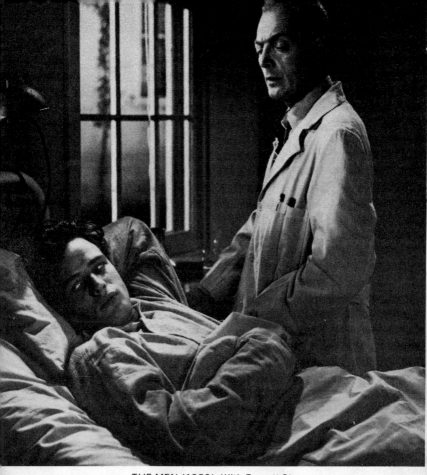

THE MEN (1950) With Everett Sloane.

tear-jerking cues in Dimitri Tiomkin's score. Within this rigged construction, Brando is cold, sullen, unsentimental, often playing recklessly against the grain of the scenes and making them doubly moving because he steadfastly refuses to budge an inch or soften an edge.

In 1950 *The Men* was considered a semi-documentary with a message of tolerance for the problems of partly incapacitated veterans. With time Brando's performance gives it a new dimension, and when he snaps out of his regression, the sequence is stunning. First his hand clutches a pulley, then his pained face looms in close-up, and a triumph of human determination is caught, wordlessly, as the muscles start straining, coming back to life.

The Men did not rate him even a nomination for the 1950 Oscar; José Ferrer won it for *Cyrano de Bergerac*. Brando was the unpopular rebel who refused to wear ties and jackets. He alienated the powerful by calling Louella Parsons "the fat one" and Hedda Hopper "the one with the hats." When introduced to Sheilah Graham he turned to Jessica Tandy and asked: "Is she your mother?" Hollywood felt that if properly ignored he would go away like some nameless threat. There was, nonetheless, no serious consideration of another actor for the film version of *A Streetcar Named Desire*.

From the start, *Streetcar* was in grave danger of being derailed. In 1951 American movies were not

THE MEN (1950). With Teresa Wright.

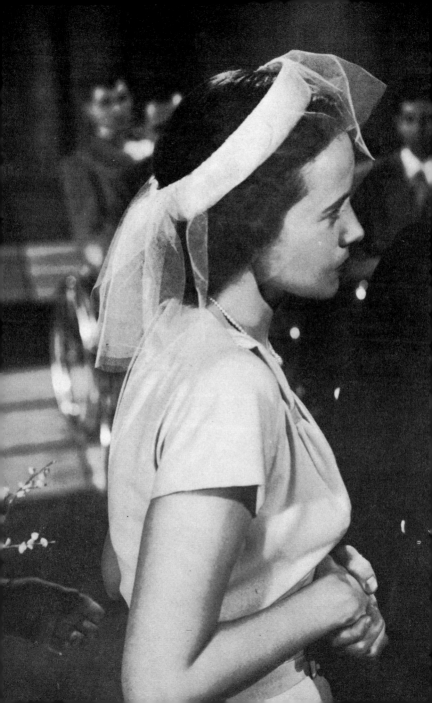

THE MEN (1950.) With Teresa Wright and Everett Sloane.

ready for the story of a woman driven to nymphomania by the suicide of her homosexual husband and then brutally raped by her brother-in-law in the steamy lower depths of New Orleans' French Quarter. Adapting the Tennessee Williams original, Oscar Saul went through dialogues with a fine-tooth comb; the protagonist, Miss DuBois, was considerably blanched, and the situation was perfect for Vivien Leigh, whose penchant for idealizing her characters was legendary. Leigh's current husband, Laurence Olivier, had directed her in the London production of the play, and she fought each of Kazan's suggestions to restore some toughness to a part that Williams had written with Tallulah Bankhead in mind.

Aided by the censors, Leigh managed to paint Blanche her favorite shade, somewhere between off-white and gleaming ivory. But she had to contend with Brando, and he cornered her into a different, unforgettable performance. The new, defenseless Blanche could easily make Kowalski into a beast pursuing a terrified prey, and Brando refused to be outmaneuvered. Method training had taught him to hunt for the truth that gives each character's worst actions their redeeming motivation. Faced with a more delicate Blanche, he reoriented his stage performance into a deeper better thought-out movi Kowalski.

Cunningly, Brando states th case for this man. He is a slob wh has married Stella, an impover ished girl of demi-aristocrati Southern background. She is sex ually beholden to his ability to "ge the colored lights going" and live the reasonably happy existence o those willing to sink below thei status. Stella and Stan have signe a peace treaty in their own privat war of the classes, with love and se cementing the *entente cordiale*.

Into this paradise of original si Blanche, the serpent, brings guil and shame. She is the accurse visiting relative, and Brando work on this point to gain audience sym pathy: with the intruder around Stella and Stan can't get "the col ored lights" going. He can't eve go to the bathroom in peace because Blanche has invaded hi most private realm by taking end less hot baths. Viscerally, Blanch is the enemy. Socially, she has th in-law vice of thinking Kowalski not good enough for her sister. Hi crudeness gives her ample ammu nition for the fight, but Brand makes sure the audience will fee that, in his own way, Stanley is a helpless as Blanche. Amid th gruffness he displays infinite ten derness for Stella, and his gesture write a subtext for the play, a

A STREETCAR NAMED DESIRE (1951). With Kim Hunter

A STREETCAR NAMED DESIRE (1951). With Vivien Leigh.

A STREETCAR NAMED DESIRE (1951). With Kim Hunter.

when he tells Stella about Blanche's lurid past, but softens the blow by hiding a soothing caress with the pretense of picking a piece of lint from her shoulder.

Like a mischievous child, Brando-Kowalski succeeds in turning the crassest boorishness into a prank. Half drunk, in a torn sweatshirt, he screams for Stella in the middle of the yard like a baying alley cat, but as she slowly comes downstairs he gives her the precious gift of the most disarmingly impish smile. Kowalski feels that something in Stella wants him to be a brute, that he appeals to a primal desire for abasement. For her fascination he puts on an apelike act and eats with his fingers, standing up, knowing that she cannot keep her hands off him.

On stage Brando's most celebrated ploy was his ability to draw other actors into his own sphere of reality, unwillingly making them play the scene his way—and surprisingly better. The trick is masterfully applied to Vivien Leigh in the rape scene. When Brando-Kowalski enters the room at night and finds Blanche-Leigh alone, he is not in the least interested in the twitchings of this half-demented woman. Stella is in the maternity ward, he is about to become a father and, jovially soused, he treats Blanche like a boozy pal in a bar, asking her to bury the hatchet

and have a drink with him.

It is she who points out, "We are to be alone," and as she cowers away from him, a look of puzzlement darkens Brando's brow. His thoughts become readable: "What does this silly woman want from me?" Suddenly all of Stanley's strutting shifts into a wordless bafflement, a shapeless fear of what is being insinuated to him, almost demanded of him. "Close the curtains before you undress any further," Leigh daintily suggests, but Brando's wary reaction makes it sound like an open carnal invitation. She has turned into the aggressor and he into the teased animal who will inevitably grow and attack.

In the play the scene ends with Kowalski telling Blanche: "Tiger, we've had this date from the beginning." The censors cut the line, but Brando makes it superfluous. His power of insinuation is such that he brings out the come-on in Leigh's delicate rejection. Throughout the film, Blanche's unconfessable motivation has been envy of Stella's sexual fulfillment and curiosity about Kowalski's "colored lights." Brando forced it into the open, enriching Leigh's performance as well as his own.

With *A Streetcar Named Desire* Hollywood accepted the inevitable, and Brando had his first nomination for an Academy Award

A STREETCAR NAMED DESIRE (1951). With Vivien Leigh.

A STREETCAR NAMED DESIRE (1951). With Kim Hunter and Vivien Leigh.

VIVA ZAPATA (1952).
As Emiliano Zapata.

His three co-stars—Leigh, Kim Hunter, and Karl Malden—received Oscars, but he was bypassed in favor of Humphrey Bogart in *The African Queen*. Brando's reputation as an *enfant terrible* was growing apace: Louella Parsons openly referred to him as "The Slob," and his innate impatience and lack of diplomacy were increasingly alienating. When a reporter asked him whether he preferred taking a bath or a shower, he replied: "Neither. I spit at the sky and run under it." He was reputedly seen driving a convertible down the Sunset Strip with an arrow broken in two and stuck half on his forehead, half on the back of his head, as if he had been hit by some improbable marksman.

How much of this is true and how much fabrication is a moot point. For years it has been argued that Brando willingly contributed to his own legend. Shelley Winters, another Actors Studio alumna, remembers visiting him on the *Streetcar* set where, after she had stepped into Brando's dressing room, he slammed the door, bolted it, and started to shake the walls. Winters claims he told her: "For God's sake, scream! Don't you want to help me build up a reputation? Scream!" He took pride in being different, and when an interviewer said, "You're just like everybody else," he ran to the corner of the room and stood on his head.

The press pounced greedily upon these stories. Brando was "hot copy," and anything that added coal to the flames was welcome. Hollywood had a new colorful character, and Stanislavskian actors were volunteering that through playing Kowalski so often Stanley had gotten under Brando's skin, like Ronald Colman's Othello in *A Double Life*. Apocryphal or not, the anecdotes made him into a household word. He was such a recognizable type that the Brando impression became a staple of cabaret acts, as one comedian after another won the easy laugh by bellowing "Stella!" in a grimy, torn, sweatshirt.

Brando could have sailed the crest of the wave and made millions as a super-stud sex symbol, but for Elia Kazan's *Viva Zapata!* (1952) the make-up department devised a new face for him to hide behind, as the Mexican revolutionary. Dark-skinned, with a bushy mustache and slanting eyelids, Brando wore an imperturbably stony Indian mask. His gaze was fixed, slightly cross-eyed, like a Mayan statue's; his countenance inscrutable as the Aztec calendar.

In the first scene Kazan's camera slides from one man to the next until it picks out Brando's Zapata in a group of peasants asking for their land rights at an audience granted by President Porfirio Díaz. Zapata, the marked man, stands apart as he openly rejects Díaz' bland paternalism. "What is your name, my son?" the dictator inquires. "Zapata, Emiliano Zapata," Brando replies, making each elastic syllable sound like a portent of tragedy.

Díaz and Zapata never meet again, but the young man's life is dedicated to the overthrow of the tyrant. Typically, in Brando's rebel there is something docile that longs for the correct kind of authority, the *good* father. It is easy for Fernando, the venomous newspaper-

VIVA ZAPATA (1952).
With Joseph Wiseman.

man (Joseph Wiseman) to sell Zapata on the idea of aligning his peasant revolt with Madero (Harold Gordon), who is plotting the revolution against Díaz in far-away Texas. Zapata has never met Madero but quickly casts him as a noble uncle.

Díaz is forced into exile, but victory is fleeting for Zapata. He finds Madero to be a weak man of ineffectual good will. Once more he rebels against authority, but it proves futile. Madero is killed by Huerta (Frank Silvera), another would-be dictator. Even Pancho Villa (Alan Reed) is a disappoint-

43

VIVA ZAPATA (1952). With his revolutionary followers.

ment: a tired sensualist who enjoyed the fighting but now longs to go home, leaving the burden of power to Zapata. He accepts it reluctantly.

For Brando's Zapata the film is a series of letdowns. The worst comes when his brother Eufemio (Anthony Quinn) is denounced by the discontented peasants as a grafter and petty tyrant. The cycle is completed and Brando—in a remarkably understated show of moral defeat—sees how neatly the wheels have turned. The scene is constructed to look like his early confrontation with Diaz, only this time Zapata is at the other side of the table.

After this, only Death and Transfiguration are possible for the warrior. With weary, suicidal stoicism, he walks into the trap set for him,

but the murderers do their job too well. The body is so riddled with bullets that the people wonder whether this unrecognizable carrion is Zapata. John Steinbeck's screenplay bogs down into heavy pseudo-folk poetry as the men say the river cannot be stopped, the wind cannot be captured, so Zapata must be hiding in the mountains, ready to come back when the people need him. At fade-out Zapata's white horse still gallops on the thin edge between superstition and mythology.

Brando is fine within the confines of the part, but it is not wide enough for his range. Kazan has often said that ambivalence is Brando's strong suit as an actor, and in the Steinbeck screenplay all the contradictions are not within him but in the situations he is

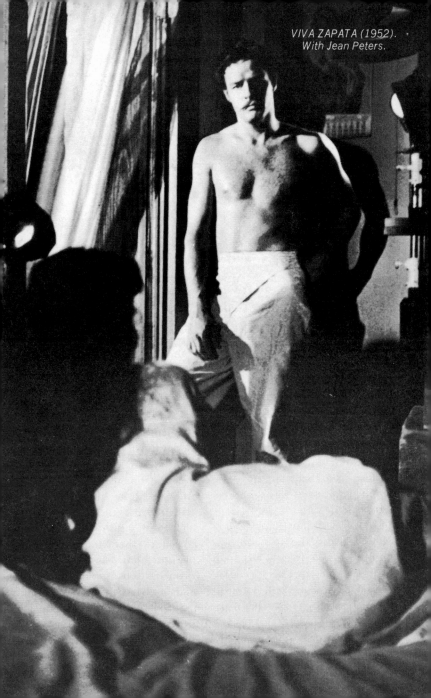

VIVA ZAPATA (1952). With Jean Peters.

forced to deal with. He only wavers once in his preordained road to martyrdom, when he decides to give up the cause and marry Josefa (Jean Peters), to whom he proposes in a hilarious exchange of proverbs, the one light touch in an oppressively fatalistic film.

Viva Zapata! illustrates one of Kazan's favorite themes—corruption through power—in such defeatist manner that a supposedly political film is really anti-political, for it implies there is no way to take a stand without being tainted. The ideological confusion was some-

what camouflaged by Kazan's effectively restless direction, but for all its sound and fury the film is static. It had the arty look of an important picture and was respectfully reviewed, won a supporting Oscar for Anthony Quinn and four additional nominations, including a second one for Brando. Mexico, rejecting this pessimistic portrait of a national hero, banned the film forever. Audiences everywhere shied away from it, and it was Brando's first box-office failure.

In 1953 the movie industry's barely disguised antagonism

xploded when MGM announced rando would play Marc Antony in heir forthcoming production of hakespeare's *Julius Caesar*. Columnists quipped that Brando ould do the part in a dirty, torn ga, mumbling his way through e speeches.

The safe, initial choices for the ole had been Leo Genn and Charlon Heston, who had played ntony in a David Bradley experiental film, but producer John Iouseman held staunchly to his riginal conception. Fifteen years efore, Houseman had produced he Mercury Theatre version of the lay, directed and acted by Orson Velles in modern dress, with deep olitical resonances uncovered and nderlined in the text.

Houseman regretted what had appened then: Welles played Brutus, and his actor's ego had onflicted with Houseman's ideas. ntony's speeches had been pared r cut, and George Coulouris dded his unctuous manner to educe the man to a cynical opporunist. Houseman longed to restore he play to his initial vision, and he new Brando was the charismatic ctor to do it. His persistence was ewarded on the day when the vorkers on the set burst into pplause after Antony's funeral oraion. Brando's righteous anger edressed the balance of the plot as e made Antony the hero and the others into arrant villains or deluded martyrs.

Julius Caesar was also a challenge for Joseph L. Mankiewicz. *A Letter to Three Wives* and *All About Eve* had won him two sets of Oscars as writer-director, and he was considered a top craftsman of a somewhat theatrical persuasion. In this incursion into the classics he would not be working with his own words but would be perilously juggling Shakespeare's.

Only a few remembered that Mankiewicz had written tough gangster films like *Manhattan Melodrama* in the thirties and directed the hard-as-nails *Somewhere in the Night* in the late forties. Within Houseman's desired framework Mankiewicz extracted the tough melodrama behind Shakespeare's play, making Brando a thrilling rabble-rouser and boldly casting Edmond O'Brien to present Casca as a two-bit punk in Roman garments.

What Houseman and Mankiewicz wanted was one thing and what MGM dreamed of was another. The studio aimed at an intellectual follow-up to *Quo Vadis*, and the sets look too clean, tidy, and stagy for the surreptitiously modern conception. Performances like Brando's and O'Brien's would have worked better in a seedy, crabby Rome, such as the one Richard Lester chose for

JULIUS CAESAR (1953).
As Marc Anthony.

JULIUS CAESAR (1953). With Louis Calhern, Greer Garson, and Deborah Kerr.

A *Funny Thing Happened on the Way to the Forum* or the one Fellini imagined for his *Satyricon.*

Julius Caesar was caught between realism and pageant, but the final flaw in the film's structure is Shakespeare's. The climax comes midway with the funeral oration, and Brando delivers an actor's coup that knocks the film out. His Antony is anything but classical. He completely disregards the meter and speaks the verse as prose, with none of the orotund tones that make this set piece a favorite high school enunciation exercise. When he shouts: "Friends, Romans, countrymen, lend me your ears," he is not an actor doing justice to a lovely cadence but an irate speaker vying for the attention of a crowd.

As soon as he has the mob in his grip, he handles it like a born demagogue. He is alternately plangent, cajoling, piercing, in a breathless crescendo. His two other speeches in the film also give him the center of the stage as they are, significantly, addressed to cadavers. He explodes in a paroxysm of rage and grief when left alone with Caesar's body, but to a dead Brutus he recites the "noblest Roman" speech with quiet tenderness and regret.

His indelible moments, nonetheless, are wordless. He shakes the bloody hands of Caesar's murderers as if he wanted to disown his whole right arm for touching these despicable men. He marks his time, swallowing hard to clear his throat after each false word of allegiance to the conspirators. A smirk of contempt curdles his lips as he turns back from the crowd he has so easily swayed. After a meeting with Octavius he stretches, as if his ambitions had become too big for his body. Then, in the film's best silent moment, he angles a bust of Caesar like a mirror in which he hopes to catch the image he is trying on for size.

Brando again imposed his sense of reality on the other players. By comparison, Louis Calhern's Caesar is pompous and John Gielgud's Cassius pallid. Only James Mason maintains an admirable balance between Brando's earthy delivery and a classical grand manner. Mankiewicz tried to unify this mixture of British theatricality, Method acting and MGM spectacle, but the film had clearly become Brando's. After his explosive tirades, the discussions between Cassius and Brutus—though abbreviated—seem dull and lifeless. And the battle of Philippi brings a decent film

JULIUS CAESAR (1953). With (left to right) Jack Raine, Edmond O'Brien, Michael Pate, Tom Powers, John Hoyt, John Gielgud, and James Mason.

JULIUS CAESAR (1953). Before the slain body of Caesar.

o a sorry conclusion by looking
uspiciously like a Comanche
mbush in a Western.

Julius Caesar won Brando his
hird Oscar nomination, and he
gain lost, to William Holden in
talag 17. Brando had acted in
ulius Caesar for a fourth of his star
tipend, and this brush with the
lassics must have spurred him to
nake, in 1953, his last theatrical
ppearance in a summer stock pro-

duction of Bernard Shaw's *Arms
and the Man*, among a company of
friends. He again talked about the
pleasures of the stage, where one
and all humbly worked toward a
common goal. But then he made
The Wild One (1954), and as a
pure, unadulterated star vehicle it
was his first bad film, his highest
plateau of popularity, and his point
of no return.

John Paxton's screenplay was

based on a real-life incident, the invasion and siege of a small town by rival motorcyclist gangs that held it under control for several hours. Laslo Benedek directed a typical Stanley Kramer production; *The Wild One* dressed its social comment with a truculence verging on caricature.

To prepare for the part, Brando rode with similar gangs, studied their behavior, and once carried his research as far as being jailed for a night. He accurately catalogued all the traits of these pseudo-rebels and proto-hoodlums. Then he colored them with his own flamboyance as a performer and came up with a fascinating, monstrous creature called Johnny. In a sociological twist, art imitated life and then life began imitating art; his near parody became paragon. Johnny-Brando begat a legion of aspiring "Wild Ones."

His first impact in the film is devastating: as he takes possession of the town's diner, the Wild One is a dangerous, barely leashed destructive force of nature. The hips are thrust forward in sexual aggression; the inner rhythm is externalized by fingers that snap to some unheard music or struggle to strike a match on a thumbnail. Every gesture is a signpost to a personal *angst* that cannot be verbalized. When it is, it becomes a mumble, as if the onrushing thoughts were smashing the structure of the sentences. The easy shrug, the tilted head, the roving eyes that can't look straight—all the elements are there, compressed into a ten-minute *tour de force* that ranks among the most excitingly theatrical entrances ever captured on film.

For the young, Johnny's hostility was all the more enticing because it was unfocused. At one point he is asked, "What are you rebelling against?" and he replies, "What have you got?" There is a whole vague superstructure oppressing Johnny, and Brando's performance established the Establishment before that catch-all concept caught on.

There are traces of Kowalski in Johnny, but Williams' character confined his disrespect to a domestic situation; *The Wild One* brought it out into open conflict with society. The equation of sex and violence is also worked out on the outside world, and Johnny's relationship with the girl (Mary Murphy) is instantly charged. Not only does she resist him, she is also the sheriff's daughter, and the Brando character takes his revenge on the figure of authority by defiling the female he most cherishes. It is a recurrent theme that Brando would later explore directly in his own *One-Eyed Jacks* and obliquely in *The Appaloosa*.

THE WILD ONE (1954). As Johnny.

THE WILD ONE (1954). With Lee Marvin and Robert Keith.

THE WILD ONE (1954). With J. C. Flippen, Robert Keith, and Mary Murphy.

THE WILD ONE (1954). *Johnny on his motorcycle.*

Like Kowalski, Johnny uses sex as a social leveler. Conquest is his aphrodisiac, and as a prelude to rape, he growls his credo at the girl: "You think you're too good for me, and when I meet people like that I knock them over." She is too exhausted and fascinated to put up a fight, but her acquiescence turns him off. "Let's go back and I'll dump you," he snarls, but she has found the chink in his armor and gains the upper hand by saying, half in wonder, half in triumph: "You are afraid of me."

She has turned the tables on Johnny and pointedly tells him that her father is a political appointee who has become the local joke because he is incapable of arresting the town bigot he owes his job to. "He's a fake, just like you," she tells Johnny, making a parallel between the sheriff's faded khaki and his own black leather outfit: they are both uniforms behind which they hide their lack of convictions. Johnny has lost the battle of the sexes, and from then on Brando sharply chronicles his disintegration.

The audience never gets to know the causes of the Wild One's hostility. This makes the film dramatically limp, but sociologically it turned it into a powerhouse. To tantalize the young, there was an evil father rattling like a skeleton in some subliminal closet; when the townsfolk give Johnny a thrashing, he groans with adolescent bravado: "My old man used to hit harder than that." Only when he escapes does he break down and weep, embracing his symbolic motorcycle. In the end he is ready for a cool, very Brandoesque act of understated half-repentance.

The Wild One is a naive, mediocre film in which each meaning is laid on with a trowel. For instance, the whole town that faces the young rebels seems to be solely inhabited by senior citizens, as if some convenient plague had killed nearly every male under fifty. Despite, or because of this, it fired people's imaginations and was praised and damned with equal fervor. Many considered it an antisocial, deleterious film, and it was banned in England until 1968.

The reaction disturbed Brando. By unmasking the existence of a social phenomenon he had popularized its most frightening, neofascist aspects. Losing control of his star power, he had aimed for horror and created glamour. For years Brando talked about "expiating" *The Wild One*. His next film, by curious coincidence, was a fable of atonement.

In *On the Waterfront* (1954), directed by Elia Kazan, he plays Terry Malloy, a not-too-bright, slightly punchy ex-boxer who lives on the edge of dockyard corruption

ON THE WATERFRONT (1954).
As Terry Malloy.

ON THE WATERFRONT (1954). With Eva Marie Saint.

and indirectly benefits from it through his brother Charlie (Rod Steiger), one of the henchmen of Mafia-like union boss Johnny Friendly (Lee J. Cobb). A young worker has dared contest Friendly's grip on the docks, and Terry is used, unknowingly, to lure him to his death. When he falls in love with Edie (Eva Marie Saint), the dead man's sister, Terry is seized with a Dostoyevskian will to confess but must choose between justice and the girl's love on the one hand and loyalty to Charlie and Friendly on the other.

With this film the symbiotic relationship between Kazan and Brando reached its productive zenith. Kazan knew that Brando could not be fenced in and that his

actor's instinct would often come up with things no one else would have discovered in the part. He let him improvise but also badgered him, coaxed him, drove him nearly to frenzy. It is his most Method-inspired performance and generally considered his best.

Brando is excellent throughout the film, but he has two especially brilliant scenes. In a bar with Edie he begins to open up and reveal his past in a children's home. He frowns as if he were looking painfully inward as he moans, "Some home . . ." Malloy is not an intelligent man, and each tormenting idea is an almost visible dot of light whirling inside his brutish head, struggling to come out. One can almost eavesdrop on his suspicious

ON THE WATERFRONT (1954). With Thomas Handley and Eva Marie Saint.

thoughts, and then, as a look of love spreads all over his face, rearranging his features into a rapture he can enjoy but not define, one is in the presence of great acting.

Later, in a taxi ride, Terry confronts Charlie with the truth that has dawned on him at last: Charlie has not played Abel but Cain; his brotherly love was never a propelling force but a deterrent. "I could have had class, I could have been a contender," Terry mutters sadly, as if apologizing for the way Charlie failed him. Then he lays the blame with a heartbreaking lack of rancor. "It was you, Charlie," he says, not even complaining. Desperate at not being able to stop Terry from testifying against Friendly, Charlie pulls a gun on him. Brando shakes his head in disbelief, gazes at Charlie like a betrayed dog and almost smiles when he whispers, "Wow," making the tritest of slang expletives sound like a Biblical lamentation.

This time the film deserved Brando's performance. Kazan had all the elements in control, from the foghorn laments that echo in Leonard Bernstein's score to the exceptional Boris Kaufman photography. The wintry light of a defeated sun bathes everything in poetic ugliness: the black, blighted houses huddled against each other, the interminable lines of empty roofs, riddled with TV antennas, the trash cans steaming in deserted lots, the people walking close to the walls, chins buried in chests, charging into the cold wind.

Kazan paces the action with the one-two punch of an expert boxer. A frenetic scene is followed by a languid one, to the climax when Brando, viciously beaten by Friendly's men, is no longer shunned as a stool pigeon by his fellow dockmen, who follow his tottering steps on the way back to work, amidst a barrage of curses from the deposed tyrant.

Both *On the Waterfront* and Brando won the New York Critics Award for best film and best actor of 1954. The film received a standing ovation at the Venice Film Festival but was ignored by the jury. A combination of the New York acco-

ON THE WATERFRONT (1954). With Karl Malden and Eva Marie Saint.

lade and the European slap made Hollywood forgive the prodigal son. Brando was at last handed an Oscar, one of the seven won by *On the Waterfront*.

He had hated the film at first sight and had stomped out of the screening room, no longer on speaking terms with Kazan. However, on the night of March 30, 1955, Hollywood saw a different man at the Academy Awards ceremony. He wore an impeccable tuxedo, exchanged quips on stage with Bob Hope, and was moved when Bette Davis embraced him and put the statuette in his shaking grip. "It's much heavier than I thought," he said beamingly. "I don't think ever in my life so many people were directly responsible for my being very, very glad."

Backstage at the Pantages Theater, Brando blinked at the flash-bulbs, embracing his co-winner, Grace Kelly. "I thought Crosby and Garland would win," he kept saying. "The sentiment was going for them." He bussed every female cheek in sight and almost kissed his arch-enemy, Louella Parsons, before both realized they were forgetting themselves.

The child in Brando loved the toy in Oscar. Many thought it would lull him into mildness and acquiescence. The wild years were over and Brando had his pacifier. They were very wrong. His time as a full-fledged star was coming, and a rebel in power is a dangerous thing.

Traditionally, stars are to be wished upon. When they are not in the sky but on the screen, the wish soon turns into the producer's command. Even before Brando won the Oscar for *On the Waterfront*, the film's success had made his name synonymous with star insurance for one expensive project after another. The financial possibilities were dizzying, and he went along for the ride. Then the carousel moved faster and faster into vertigo. Jumping down would have required the courage of a hero, the moral stamina of a saint.

During the fifties Brando tried to escape Hollywood by considering European offers. Producer Paul Graetz sued him when he withdrew from *The Red and the Black* in disagreement with director Claude Autant Lara; Gérard Philipe replaced him. Director Marc Allegret could not meet Brando's salary terms for the French version of *Lady Chatterley's Lover* and chose Erno Crisa instead. Most interesting of all, Luchino Visconti conceived *Senso* for Brando and Ingrid Bergman but financial hurdles made him settle for Farley Granger and Allida Valli. Grudgingly but profitably, Brando stayed in California.

His next six films after *On the Waterfront* were adaptations of hit plays or best sellers, not to mention the equally high-powered vehicles

THE STAR YEARS

he turned down, such as Otto Preminger's *The Man with the Golden Arm*, King Vidor's *War and Peace*, and Vincente Minnelli's *The Four Horsemen of the Apocalypse*. Brando was fighting against insurmountable pressures; in 1954, his brush with *The Egyptian* seemed like an isolated incident in his career, but it was symptomatic of what the next decade held in store for him.

Brando had liked the first draft of the screenplay, based on a popular novel by Mika Waltari. He arrived at 20th Century-Fox for a reading of the finished script. The director was Michael Curtiz, and Brando's co-star would be Bella Darvi, Darryl F. Zanuck's current protegée. Realizing that much empty pageantry had been added to the original to insure spectacular values, Brando proclaimed *The Egyptian* "a camel opera." He could not stand Curtiz and much less Darvi, so he fled to New York where his psychiatrist, Dr. Bela Mittelbaum, got him out of the predicament by informing the studio that Brando was "a very sick and mentally confused boy."

Brando was accused of malingering, though for a sensitive, serious actor the prospect of playing *The*

DESIREE (1954). As Napoleon Bonaparte.

DESIREE (1954). With Merle Oberon.

Egyptian against Darvi could have been depressing indeed. In the mid-fifties, stars just didn't walk out on multimillion-dollar projects. Fox indignantly sued Brando for two million dollars, and Zanuck gave his role to Edmund Purdom.

The underlying irony is that *The Egyptian*, under Curtiz' muscular direction, turned out to be somewhat better than *Desirée*, the cream-puff romance with which Brando eventually paid his debt to the studio. Curtiz was an underrated craftsman, but he was also famous as the most difficult of directors until Otto Preminger inherited his title of resident movie ogre. The clash between Curtiz and Brando would have been apocalyptic, to say the least. He got *Desirée* and Henry Koster instead.

An affable, charming man, Koster had made his fame and fortune by directing several of Deanna Durbin's hits. Despite his reputation as a dispenser of saccharine-coated fantasies, he was by no means an incompetent director of actors and later got fine performances out of more cooperative stars like James Stewart in *Mr. Hobbs Takes a Vacation*, Marlene Dietrich in *No Highway in the Sky*, and Dana Wynter in *The Sixth of June*. But Koster lacked the strength or perseverance to cope with Brando. The director brought his ample collection of Napoleonic art to the set and placed a bust of Bonaparte in Brando's dressing room, the better to inspire him to play his own vision of Napoleon. The star did not respond to the soothing treatment, and *Desirée* is widely regarded as the first film in which Brando directed himself.

Desirée is a rosy movie version of a best seller by Annemarie Selinko, revolving around Napoleon's first love, the girl who eventually reigned in Sweden as Bernadotte's wife. Unable to make headway with Brando, Koster concentrated on Jean Simmons, who played the title role. Slyly, Koster turned the picture into a latter-day version of a Durbin vehicle, especially *Spring Parade*, in which Durbin enchanted Emperor Franz Joseph in much the same manner the fetching Simmons conquered Bonaparte. Merle Oberon's subtle performance as the aging, discarded Josephine drove the film further into the "woman's picture" category. Brando was left to contend with Napoleon, a certifiably unplayable part that had defeated Charles Boyer and later eluded Daniel Gélin, Raymond Pellegrin, Herbert Lom, and Rod Steiger, among others.

It was a lost cause, but Brando fought to give Napoleon as much credibility as the Daniel Taradash screenplay allowed. His option to play the role with a British accent is

DESIREE (1954). With Jean Simmons.

a good defensive ploy; he is different and foreign enough, without attempting a French manner that could have made him sound like a maître d' in a posh bistro. "I let the make-up play it," he said after finishing *Desirée*, a film in which he is less tackling a role than avoiding ridicule.

After a shockingly bad start he grows into the part. It is evident that the triumphant, romantic Napoleon is not one of his heroes, so he plays him negatively, as if Bonaparte despised himself and scorned all the pomp and circumstance that made him "the man of destiny." When he crowns himself in Notre Dame cathedral, a disdainful Brando seems to be rehearsing for self-decapitation.

This eccentric reading makes the first half of *Desirée* very awkward, but it pays generously toward the end, as the façade crumbles and the man emerges. When a defeated Napoleon returns for a last encounter with Desirée, Brando reaps all the seeds of discontent he had planted, playing the scene with a mixture of sated ego and infinite boredom that saves the film for him as an actor.

Brando was ready to go out on a

limb again with *Guys and Dolls* (1955), the film version of the Broadway musical, directed by another daring experimentalist, Joseph L. Mankiewicz. As Sky Masterson, the Runyonesque raffish gambler, Brando was miscast. Comedy has never been his forte, and he is always most amusing when his characters are not supposed to be funny, as in the first half of *Streetcar* or the marriage proposal scene in *Viva Zapata!* Trying for laughs in *Guys and Dolls*, his lightest touch is a karate chop.

He is at his best with Jean Simmons, who plays the Salvation Army doll with severe tenderness, and at his worst with Frank Sinatra, equally miscast as Nathan Detroit, a part that demands the quality of Jewish wry Sam Levene had on stage. Sinatra made no effort to hide the fact that it was Brando's role he coveted, and indeed he would have been a perfect Sky Masterson. He called Brando "Mr. Mumbles, the most overrated actor in the world." Brando countered by saying that when Sinatra went to Heaven he would yell at God for making him bald. An intense rivalry developed between them, and their scenes together seem like duets to the tune of "Everything

GUYS AND DOLLS (1955). As gambler Sky Masterson, with Frank Sinatra at right.

GUYS AND DOLLS (1955). With Jean Simmons.

GUYS AND DOLLS (1955). With Vivian Blaine.

you can do I can do cuter." In their battle of coyness even stern Mankiewicz was unable to referee.

As Masterson, Brando aimed at a loosening of his image, and at least he had a chance to sing and dance pleasantly, as if no harm were intended. *Guys and Dolls* was a letdown in comparison with its Broadway counterpart, mostly because Mankiewicz's direction never found an adequate compromise between the fey and the realistic. When Brando sang to Simmons about the need for "chemistry" in life, he was indirectly pointing at

the missing link between the stars, the director, and the material.

If *Guys and Dolls* was a challenge, Brando's next one, *The Teahouse of the August Moon* (1956), was a mad gamble against all odds. Sakini, the Okinawan interpreter for American occupation troops, was dreamed up as an elfin, gnomelike figure. He had been originally played on Broadway by David Wayne, an Actors Studio graduate who had triumphed as the leprechaun in *Finian's Rainbow*. Sakini begs for such a winsome, small-framed

GUYS AND DOLLS (1955). With Jean Simmons.

GUYS AND DOLLS (1955). With Frank Sinatra, Vivian Blaine, Jean Simmons, and Regis Toomey.

actor that the role was even played by a woman, Rosita Díaz Jimeno, in a Spanish touring production organized by Jean Dalrymple. Brawny, sexy Brando just could not compress himself into Sakini.

John Patrick adapted his own play into film, and *The Teahouse of the August Moon* opens with Brando-Sakini speaking directly to the camera. Soliloquy is Brando's forte, and for a few minutes it seems the experiment is going to work out, as he faces the movie audience, sitting tailorwise with a smile on his lips and a twinkle in his eyes. He winks as he displays a chewing gum trophy—"Tutti frutti, gift from American soldier" —and Sakini emerges as the eter-

nal picaresque hero in a colonial tableau, a man for whom Occupation is occupational.

The make-up is astounding, from the almond eyes to the gapped teeth. The accent is playfully, not heavily mocked as Sakini collides with treacherous R's and ellides them to proclaim himself "rife with *rife.*" It is a very promising monologue—and the only one he has until the very end. The screenplay eschewed the play's fantasy framework, and as soon as Sakini loses firsthand contact with the audience, Brando becomes desperately arch.

His body is against him. The Brando slouch turns into Sakini's crouch as he tries to hide his corpu-

THE TEAHOUSE OF THE JGUST MOON (1956). As Sakini.

THE TEAHOUSE OF THE AUGUST MOON (1956). With Glenn Ford.

lence by pushing his torso forward, letting his hands dangle in an ape-like posture. Instead of a freshly unbottled genie, he is a punch-drunk, Oriental Terry Malloy. Pregnant pauses often deliver still-born lines, as when he is asked by the American major: "Where is your get up and go?" Brando wonders a second too long, ponders a measure too deep before he comes back with: "I guess my get up and go ... went." So does the guffaw.

The adaptation deprived him of his role as Brechtian raconteur and chorus, and in the movie Sakini is little more than a supporting part.

Glenn Ford, Machiko Kyo, Eddie Albert, and Paul Ford were all at their professional best; Brando was less and less the focus of attention. His predicament can be observed in a scene where Glenn Ford is making a telephone call while Brando and Albert are passively waiting it out. Albert, after years of training as a dependable supporting actor, plays it in a subdued manner and makes his presence felt without outwardly competing with Ford. Brando fidgets, over-reacts and mugs in needless and distracting pantomime.

More than scene-stealing, it is sheer rejection of inactivity, yet

THE TEAHOUSE OF THE AUGUST MOON (1956). With (left to right) Eddie Albert, Glenn Ford, Paul Ford, and Harry Morgan.

THE TEAHOUSE OF THE AUGUST MOON (1956). With Glenn Ford and Machiko Kyo.

SAYONARA (1957). As Major Lloyd Grover.

Brando's attempts to save an ever-diminishing role irked his co-stars, and columns were full of reports of a flaming feud between him and Glenn Ford. All the friction was in vain, for the film is stolen by the other Ford, Paul, who assumed his original stage role as the bumbling major after Louis Calhern died in mid-shooting. It was petty larcen though, for *Teahouse* is like th Japanese crushed paper flowe that bloom again in a bowl of wat Under Daniel Mann's arid dir tion, it shriveled in the drought.

With *Sayonara* (1957) Bran started his long campaign to some moral satisfaction out of t films his presence insured at the box-office. According to Harold Clurman, his director in *Truckline Café*, Brando rationalized a reluctance to come back to the theater by believing he could reach a wider audience in films and exert a more powerful influence in presenting his ideals. It was in this mood that he accepted *Sayonara*; he felt the James Michener novel of interracial romance gave him an opportunity to say something important about prejudice in its many forms.

With the encouragement of producer-director Joshua Logan,

SAYONARA (1957). With Patricia Owens.

SAYONARA (1957). With Miiko Taka.

Brando rewrote the whole screenplay to suit his point of view, but of his extensive revisions no more than half a dozen pages remained. There were too many potential toes to be stepped on, and to gain the vital cooperation of the Air Force, Logan had to camouflage the fact that American servicemen who married Japanese women were quietly removed from their posts and sent back home.

When Brando found out all his suggestions had been discarded, his idealism curdled into sour cynicism. He arrived in Japan with a full star retinue that included his own private make-up man. He

began downgrading *Sayonara* even while it was shooting and told Truman Capote that he had mugged and eye-rolled in one scene just to see how far Logan would let him go, yet the director had gladly shouted: "Print it."

Like many of Brando's public statements the *Sayonara* stories have to be taken with a generous pinch of salt. There is no eye rolling or excess in this performance, one of his most subdued. His Air Force major is a touching innocent abroad, teetering between righteousness and compassion. One of the few Brando ideas that remain in the film is his oice to make the protagonist a xan, to emphasize the angle of uthern prejudice. He imitates e accent to the last twang as each yer of irrational prejudice is ipped away from the character en he falls in love with the Japase girl (Miiko Taka).

Brando complained that the role as too passive, and his best scene as shot against his will. Red Butns and Miyoshi Umeki, the rassed interracial couple, comit suicide; Brando wanted to have iolent, passionate outburst as he and their bodies. Logan thought fferently, but appeased the star by agreeing to shoot both versions. Logan had Brando walking through a mute crowd of Japanese until he comes upon his dead friends. He stops, moves his hand as if trying to erase it all, and whispers: "Oh, no." From the first take it was so effective that Brando conceded the point; his version was not filmed.

Sayonara won nine Academy Award nominations, including one for best picture. Both Brando and Logan were up for Oscars, and the movie won four, for cinematography and art direction as well as for Red Buttons and Miyoshi Umeki. The disputed screenplay,

SAYONARA (1957). With Martha Scott and Kent Smith.

SAYONARA (1957). With Red Buttons.

credited to Paul Osborn, was also nominated.

The bite had been carefully extracted from *Sayonara*, and the lovers do not say goodbye as in the novel's ending, making the title inoperative. Brando had been intransigent about his, but what he thought of as a statement of belief came out as a happy ending that guaranteed a box-office success. On its fairy tale level the film works well enough, but this visually beguiling, fifties-style *Madame Butterfly* was hardly Brando's cup of sake.

Brando's life often curiously parallels his films, and after *Sayonara* he married Anna Kashfi, an Indian girl from Calcutta. In October 1957 he was in Arizona scouting locations for a Western he planned to produce and that eventually turned into *One-Eyed Jacks*. Thinking the state laws banned this mixed union, he flew to California where the couple exchanged vows in an Indian ceremony, she in a sari while he held a pearl in his fingers.

Shortly after the wedding, newspapermen dug into Kashfi's background and found out she was Joanna O'Callaghan, a Welsh girl from Cardiff with rather tenuous claims to an Indian mystique. Brando kept silent through the chorus of Hollywood snickers, but the marriage was doomed. He divorced Kashfi soon after their

son, Christian Devi, was born. F the next 14 years, the couple we in and out of court, fighting ov custody of the child in highly pub cized battles.

These personal troubles we further complicated by care problems. The neurotic anti-he Brando had brought to the scre had been taken further, into ne psychosis, by the performances scores of neo-Brandos such as V Morrow in *The Blackboard Jung* and John Cassavetes and Ma Rydell in *Crime in the Streets*. Th prime example of the Brandoesq leading man was James Dea whose meteoric career ended death.

Like Frankenstein, Brando w concerned about the movie mo sters he had spawned. At a party l tried to dissuade Dean from h self-destructive course, and in 19 he toyed with the idea of playir film coroner in Dean's post morte by doing the narration of Robe Altman's documentary, *The Jam Dean Story*.

All around him everybody w playing Brando, and he had to pl somebody else. He welcomed ar film that gave him a chance to l different, and *The Young Lior* (1958) served this purpose—up a point. Another Brando trait w established with this film: he wou not play villains. Brando once sa that if he walked into a room an

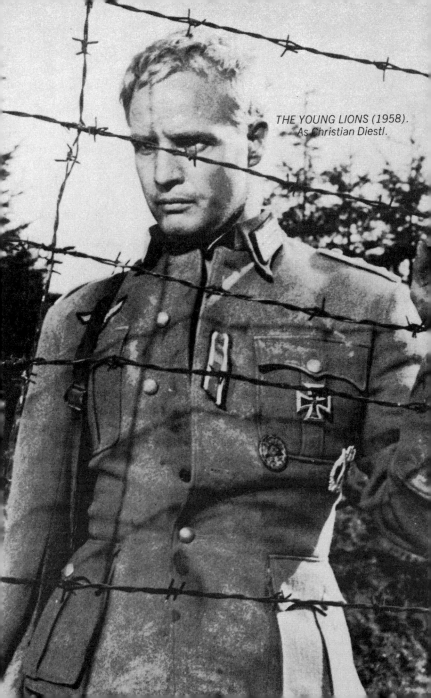

THE YOUNG LIONS (1958).
As Christian Diestl.

THE YOUNG LIONS (1958). With Maximilian Schell.

one person in a hundred hated him, he felt ill at ease and walked out as soon as possible. The vehicles he chose or revamped indicate that he also could not face the hatred of an audience. In *The Young Lions* he was to play Christian Diestl, the evil Nazi, but a private Nuremberg trial was convoked in a hectic script conference,

and Diestl was considerably denazified in the film.

Irwin Shaw's novel has a three-way plot that follows a ruthless German, a wary Jew, and a blithely unconcerned regular American guy to a contrived crossroads: the complaisant Yank witnesses the death of the Jew Ackerman and becomes his avenger by exterminating the brutal Diestl. In Edward Anhalt's screenplay Diestl undergoes such a drastic change of heart that Shaw indignantly disclaimed any relation to the picture and refused to see it.

Whatever the author's objections this time Brando was right. His Christian Diestl is a richer, far more interesting character than the book's one-dimensional villain. He plays him as a social climber who dons the olive green of Hitler's army to get ahead in a stratified society, thus changing a rather clumsy book into a World War II version of Stendhal's *The Red and the Black*, in which Julien Sorel has to choose between the black robe of a priest or the red Napoleonic uniform.

In Nazi Germany, Diestl's choice is even more limited, but like Sorel in the classic French novel, he is a con man with a conscience, a go-getter doomed from the word go. He is dazzled by his sudden preeminence but is quickly revolted by its cost in blood. The screenplay constantly puts him to the test. Intoxicated with his glamorous position, he tangles with May Britt to the sinuous pandering of a saxophone. He is bedazzled by an ultra-Nazi (Maximilian Schell), who takes Diestl for a motorcycle ride through the North African front, in

THE YOUNG LIONS (1958). With May Britt.

THE YOUNG LIONS (1958). With Maximilian Schell.

a Mephistophelean tour of Rommel country.

As the film progresses, each of these scenes is harshly deflated. Schell, the Aryan prototype, becomes a human wreck who begs Diestl for a bayonet to end his misery. The sexy interlude with Britt is caricatured in an encounter with another, famished woman, who uses sex not for pleasure but for food.

All through the shifting moods Brando moves with the nervous elegance of the in-between man. Each military bow is brief enough

to offer and withdraw allegiance at the same time; each reply is weighed for its pros and cons. His words are miserly, minted coin by niggardly coin in a phonetic mutation of German speech into English, punctuated by a rhetorical "eh?" that gives Diestl time to think what to say next, since the slightest miscalculation can ruin him.

Brando's Diestl is a Reichstag Lucifer, but the actor was determined to be more than a fallen angel. He insisted that his character achieve sainthood through martyrdom. *The Young Lions* concludes with Diestl facing the horror of a concentration camp, the ultimate price of his worldly ambitions. Brando wanted the film to end with a shot of him spreadeagled on the makeshift cross of a barbed wire fence. It was difficult to get his way in a film that was split between him, Montgomery Clift, and Dean Martin. The latter was innocuous in a role diluted first in the writing, then in the editing. There was still Clift, Brando's co-student at the Actors Studio and his only serious rival as America's best actor of their generation. Clift objected strongly to the final crucifixion of Brando, and he won the point. Brando merely fingers the wire but dies less symbolically. At the time someone said: "No one gets to play Jesus in a movie if Clift is in it."

Brando's rivalries with Sinatra and Ford had fragmented *Guys and Dolls* and *Teahouse*, but *The Young Lions* gained from his acting competition with Clift, since they have no scenes together but alternate for the center of the arena like bullfighters in a *mano-a-mano*. They come to a draw, but the film won. Despite its inconsistencies, *The Young Lions* is still an exciting showcase for exceptional acting.

The film received mixed reviews and so did Brando's performance, but his mind was already focused on something else. For a long time Brando had been working on the first production to be undertaken by his own company, named Pennebaker in memory of his mother's maiden name. The film was initially known as "A Touch of Vermilion" and changed titles several times before it was officially called *One-Eyed Jacks*.

The project started innocently enough when producer Frank P. Rosenberg bought the rights to Charles Neider's novel, *The Authentic Death of Hendry Jones*. At the time every other film-in-progress was sent initially to Brando for a quick rejection, and Rosenberg did just that—part joke, part superstition, part tradition. To his surprise the book came back in three days with Brando's approval.

Six weeks were scheduled for completion of the screenplay, a job that took eight months. Calder Willingham, a fine ribald novelist and able screenwriter, worked on it for a while and quit after his efforts repeatedly clashed with Brando's requirements. Guy Trosper succeeded him, and the situation got worse. When Brando went to Japan to make *Sayonara*, he took the unfinished script along and worked on it steadily.

He came back with a tentative version and a director was named: Stanley Kubrick, the promising young man who had built a reputation and a cult with *The Killing* and *Paths of Glory*. A lonely house on top of a hill was rented for the occasion and an uneasy quartet gathered around the swimming pool for the completion of "A Touch of Vermilion's" shooting script.

Producer Rosenberg, writer Trosper, director Kubrick, and actor Brando argued the fine points of the story. Brando was self-appointed referee, and he struck a gong every time the arguments got heated or pointless. After some time, according to Brando, Kubrick confessed that he had no idea what the movie was all about. "It's about the $350,000 we've already spent," Brando replied. Kubrick bailed out when Kirk Douglas offered him a chance to replace Anthony Mann as the director of *Spartacus*, another troubled film. Brando assumed direction of "A Touch of Vermilion."

All through the story conference period, Brando had been rounding up the cast. In Mexico he signed a young actress, Pina Pellicer, and set her up in a Beverly Hills hotel to learn English phonetically. Karl Malden and Katy Jurado were also hired, and fretful about the postponements. All were on salary, escalating the film's pre-production budget into a sizable figure.

Cameras rolled at last on December 2, 1958, and the pattern was soon set. Brando was trying to direct the film in the Stanislavskian manner. In the scene where he is lashed by Karl Malden, Brando cued the extras to think of all the terrible things in their pasts, so "the camera will photograph the horror in your faces." He offered a $350 bonus for the most horrified expression. None of these close-ups is in the final print, but the anecdote suggests why a film scheduled for 60 days went on for six months. The Brando system was not silly, just impractical; he was not Stella Adler painstakingly coaching students but a man with an expensive location expenditure mushrooming every minute.

The filming started leisurely and ended frantically. *One-Eyed Jacks* resembled a gently simmering *haute cuisine* dish hastily transferred to a pressure cooker because the dinner guests are already at the door. Several links were missing in the editing, so a year and a half after the film was officially finished the cast had to be reassembled for additional scenes, including a bittersweet ending the studio insisted upon.

Editing started all over again. According to the studio, there were a quarter of a million feet, and the film ran 35 hours, a press agent's hyperbole worthy of Eisenstein's fabled *Que Viva Mexico*. At any

ONE-EYED JACKS (1961). With Karl Malden.

rate, the print Brando approved ran about five hours and was drastically hacked down to two hours and twenty minutes. Whole subplots were scuttled, including a romantic interlude with an Oriental actress named Lisa Lu, as the girl who shelters the wounded Brando in a quaint seaside village inhabited by Chinese fishermen. This costly set is barely used in the film and Lisa Lu disappeared, but all the unused material raised the final cost to five million dollars.

The creative anguish over *One-Eyed Jacks* is baffling in view of its very simple plot: In Sonora, circa 1885, Rio (Brando) and Dad Longworth (Karl Malden) are outlaws on the run after robbing a bank; Dad betrays Rio the Kid, who spends five years rotting in jail; he escapes, seething with revengeful fury, and tracks down Dad, now a respectable Monterey sheriff with a wife (Katy Jurado) and step-daughter Luisa (Pina Pellicer).

Rio's vendetta turns sexual as he

ONE-EYED JACKS (1961). With Pina Pellicer.

deliberately seduces Luisa. The sheriff finds out and gives him a public thrashing, but when Rio is about to come back to kill Dad, Luisa dissuades him. He is willing to forgive Dad, but the older man shoots first and Rio kills him. In the original ending Rio also dies, but in the revised finale he promises the pregnant Luisa to return some day.

Why did Brando spend so much time, money, and energy on this? There has been plenty of guess-work and much clutching at Freudian straws to interpret *One-Eyed Jacks* as an Oedipal fantasy between Dad and the Kid, or as a political allegory of duplicity in high places. Brando's explanation for his title is in the face men show in public life, with an ugly, hidden profile in the reverse.

The star-director perversely shot down most of the fanciful speculation as he became his own film's worst enemy by treating it like the beloved child that comes off less brilliantly than his parent expected. Brando had started by defining *One-Eyed Jacks* as "a frontal assault on the temple of clichés," but by the time it was released he was referring to it as "a potboiler." "Very conventional," he said of it. "I spent three years on it and became fond of it. It's like spending a long time building a chicken coop. When it's finished one wants to feel it hasn't been a waste of time."

One-Eyed Jacks is neither a potboiler nor a chicken coop. It is also far from being a work of art. Charles Lang beautifully photographed this self-conscious, lyrical Western, and director Brando, despite his ponderous straining for something meaningful, was best in the action sequences: the two bank robberies, the bar brawl with Timothy Carey, and the last gunfight with Malden are excitingly shot and paced.

The film has many fine images and ideas: Dad's horizontal body in a hammock as Rio's silhouette ominously appears in the distance; Elisha Cook grimacing like a nervous, trapped chipmunk in his bank teller's cage, just about to pull a gun on the bandits; Luisa's seduction on a quiet beach, intercut with a raucous fiesta. Brando's disregard for the dramatic value of words is evident in the way gestures and looks convey the meanings in the two main scenes between Jurado and Pellicer. The women speak Spanish throughout, but no knowledge of the language is necessary to get across the important plot points: that Rio made love to the girl and that she is pregnant.

Brando's direction of actors is faultless. Malden and Ben Johnson are splendid, and Katy Jurado has never been better. From Pina Pellicer he drew a lovely, fragile performance she could never equal; the actress committed suicide in Mexico a few years later. The only one Brando was unable to direct was himself. This is his poorest performance, magnified by frequent and awkward close-ups, sabotaged by unspeakable lines such as: "You are the most decent woman I know" or "I learned my manners in barrooms, senora."

Except for a few critics who were sympathetic to its erratic values, *One-Eyed Jacks* was dismissed as a vanity film and an exercise in actor's megalomania. Personally hurt, Brando declared he was not an artist but a businessman, that movies were not art anyway, and that he felt his career was coming to an end. In two years, he claimed, he would retire to devote his full time to writing. If the reaction seems overly emotional, it must be taken into account that *One-Eyed Jacks* was the second of two costly failures in a row.

Brando's next film, *The Fugitive Kind* (1960) was made while *One-Eyed Jacks* was being re-edited. It

ONE-EYED JACKS (1961). With Katy Jurado, Karl Malden, and Pina Pellicer.

ONE-EYED JACKS (1961). Directing on the set, with Miriam Colon and Karl Malde

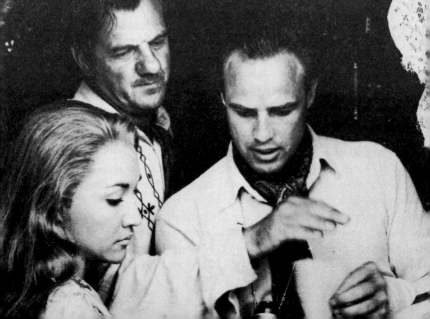

was a project Brando never wanted to join. Tennessee Williams had written the play, *Orpheus Descending*, with Brando and Anna Magnani in mind, but she had been wary of her poor English and he of the sketchy part of Val Xavier. Maureen Stapleton and Cliff Robertson had played the roles on Broadway, and the show was coldly received. When the film version was in the planning stage, Brando became the first actor ever to be offered a million dollars for a picture.

He was in no financial position to refuse. *One-Eyed Jacks* had put Pennebaker Productions well into the red, and Brando, Sr., had been ill-advised to invest his son's capital in a cattle ranch venture that collapsed. The Kashfi divorce was an added drain. Brando had married Movita, the Mexican actress who had played Gable's native girl in the 1935 version of *Mutiny on the Bounty* and now had two children by her, Sergio and Rebecca. His pressing personal obligations forced him to make the wrong career decision; he had no option but to accept *The Fugitive Kind*.

It was by no means a shoddy enterprise. Williams had adapted his own play (with Meade Roberts), and the director was Sidney Lumet, a member of the Actors Studio's first privileged nucleus, who had distinguished himself as a television director and had gone successfully into films with *Twelve Angry Men*. Magnani and Joanne Woodward, both recent Oscar winners, were Brando's co-stars.

From his first reading of the play Brando had felt the man's part was weak, unformed, and unplayable except by attitudinizing. His suspicions were right. In rehearsals before the shooting started, Lumet realized the Brando character almost disappeared in the last half of the story. Hastily, Lumet offered solutions to Williams, who could never rewrite the role into any dramatic cohesion. As Lumet has said, it is very hard to do *Orpheus Descending* without Orpheus, yet Williams had written a much stronger woman protagonist, and no amount of last-minute revisions solved the problem.

In *The Fugitive Kind* Brando plays Val Xavier, a drifter of obscure origins who arrives at a small town and gets a job in a store run by Lady Torrence (Anna Magnani), a sex-starved woman whose husband (Victor Jory) is dying of cancer upstairs. Val is pursued by Carol (Joanne Woodward), the enigmatic local tramp-of-good-family, who covets his snakeskin jacket as much as his body and tries to seduce him in the cemetery. Val is more attracted to the mature Lady and gets her pregnant. The dying husband shoots her and sets fire to the

THE FUGITIVE KIND (1960). With Anna Magnani.

THE FUGITIVE KIND (1960). With Anna Magnani.

THE FUGITIVE KIND (1960). With Joanne Woodward.

store, and the irate townfolk force Val to die, open-armed and Christlike, amid the flames.

The screenplay, blessed with Williams's gift for words, is far better than any brief synopsis suggests, but Lumet's portentous direction eliminates the positive and accentuates the negative. Brando ambles around like a poeticized Kowalski, playing against an almost unintelligible Magnani and a freakishly made-up Woodward. He has his moments, notably when left alone at the start in an interrogation by unseen judges neatly gleaned from *Rashomon.* But this was not his film, and he never should have made it. The same applies, in spades, to his next picture, *Mutiny on the Bounty* (1962).

Aaron Rosenberg, a successful producer of Anthony Mann-James Stewart Westerns at Universal, had moved to MGM and wanted a big-budget spectacular to prove his mettle in the more affluent and permissive studio. Director John Sturges came up with the idea of remaking *Mutiny on the Bounty,* the 1935 MGM Oscar winner, as a vehicle for Brando, either in the Fletcher Christian part that Gable had played or as the cruel Captain Bligh that Laughton had made memorable.

If Brando could have been persuaded to be an unredeemable villain, he would have been a remarkable Bligh, but Rosenberg played safe with the star system and offered him the part of Christian. He turned it down flat. Early in 1960 Rosenberg commissioned a screenplay from Eric Ambler and, undaunted, sent the finished first draft to Brando. This time the star was receptive—with reservations.

Brando was interested in the latter part of Nordhoff and Hall's *Bounty* trilogy, where the mutineers are given paradise on earth in Pitcairn Island but manage to turn it into a hell of greed and mistrust. Rosenberg agreed to the suggested changes and two additional writers were hired for the script: Borden Chase and William Briskill. Brando accepted, and the film was scheduled to start on October 1, 1960.

When that date arrived, the revised screenplay was far from completed, but a $750,000 motor-equipped reproduction of the ship was in construction. Pressures were mounting for an immediate start. The film had been budgeted at about six million dollars, and a sharp Damoclean sword was hanging over everyone's head.

As soon as he had been approached by Rosenberg, Brando had refused to play Christian as Gable had: a rough, practical guy turned reluctant hero. He did not want to fight nostalgia with the wrong choice of weapons. His

MUTINY ON THE BOUNTY (1962). As Fletcher Christian.

MUTINY ON THE BOUNTY (1962). With Trevor Howard.

Christian was to be high-minded, aristocratic, intellectual, and a stern adherent to a gentleman's code. In Brando's suggested version Christian despised Bligh as the crude, uneducated man who has risen to his rank on a no-nonsense basis, tinged with opportunistic brutality. Theirs was to be a subtle bout between opposing classes.

All the psychological twists were still unsolved in the screenplay, but the film was rushed into production, with Carol Reed directing, Trevor Howard as Bligh, and Richard Harris as John Adams. The first three months were catastrophic, with Brando demanding the new screenplay he had been promised and angrily finding himself playing scenes that belonged in the rejected first draft. The fully rigged *Bounty* had arrived late, and the rainy season in

Tahiti started before much of the vital footage was completed.

Production stopped and the company was called back to Hollywood to retrench. Carol Reed was replaced by Lewis Milestone, and the screenplay was entrusted to Charles Lederer, who received full credit for it even after several others had a finger in this crow stuffed pie. Brando was still unhappy with the new script. When shooting resumed, he was hardly on speaking terms with Rosenberg and Milestone. The film went on and on, for a final count of two years and an alleged cost of 20 million dollars. *Mutiny on the Bounty* was the sort of comedy of errors or tragedy of misjudgment in which everyone's behavior is easy to understand and difficult to defend. Rosenberg wanted to save his reputation and the heavy MGM

96

investment. Trevor Howard and Richard Harris wanted to leave this interminable movie and go on to desperately delayed commitments. Milestone was defending his prestige as a strict professional, and Brando was fighting for a comeback role after two consecutive flops.

The basic problem was that Milestone, the Oscar-winning veteran director of *All Quiet on the Western Front*, was the wrong man to deal with Brando's style. Every suggestion the actor made to enrich his character was rejected. Each time Milestone said "Just do it," Brando countered with "Why?" The motivation for Christian had changed midway in the script scramble, and Brando knew the insincerity would show in close-ups. Milestone even accused him of stuffing his ears with cotton to avoid hearing the director's instructions.

The showdown came with the Pitcairn Island sequence. It was still to be written to anyone's satisfaction, and from this point on the *Bounty* story is a matter of conjecture. Brando is supposed to have written a 20-minute sequence that was considered unfilmable by Milestone and Rosenberg, so Ben Hecht was called in as script doctor for the agonizing film. Brando played the Hecht version with such lack of interest that it had to be discarded. Billy Wilder is also mentioned as the author of still another conclusion.

What really happened is an enigma, but the most widely circulated version is that Brando took a leave of absence from Thailand, where he was already filming *The Ugly American*, and came back for retakes of what was called "the eighth ending." Milestone fulfilled his contract by being present but only in his dressing room reading magazines.

Columnists reaped the wild wind blowing around the *Bounty*. The anecdotes were so juicy that most were printed without checking their accuracy, and now the *Bounty* saga sounds suspiciously like the creation of Hollywood publicists trying to preserve an image of corporate sanity before the MGM stockholders. In the wake of the debacle MGM stock dropped ten points, and the anti-Brando press was having a field day with stories about the distressed studio under siege by the unreasonable actor.

Milestone summed it all up when he said that the last days of the *Bounty* were like a ship in a storm, without a pilot or a compass. He blamed the studio for not having the guts to make Brando accept their strictures or quit. But Milestone was also fair enough to add that, at bottom, Brando was right: "He was too intelligent and sensitive to play the part as Gable did."

MUTINY ON THE BOUNTY (1962). With Tarita.

Inevitably *Mutiny on the Bounty* is not one film but three distinct ones, with a different Brando in each. He starts the movie boldly, as a comedy of manners, with Christian arriving aboard ship in a crimson velvet cape, mincing around as foppishly as Douglas Fairbanks Sr. or Tyrone Power in both the silent and sound versions of *The Mark of Zorro*. Brando overdoes the effeminacy, presumably to trap Bligh into discounting him as a weakling, but the scenes are an isolated setting for a confrontation that never develops along these lines.

The comedy becomes risqué upon their arrival in Tahiti, when Bligh orders Christian to keep his hands off the native princess (Tarita) and then finds out that her father, the native chief, is offended by this slight on his daughter. Bligh fumingly gives his first mate permission to make love to the girl, and Brando prepares himself by lewdly skinning a banana before sailing ashore with a triumphant smirk, to the martial tune of "Rule Britannia."

This racy introduction proves a liability as soon as the second *Bounty* gets underway. The mood darkens and Brando suddenly abandons his foppish manner — and most of his upper-class British accent — as he rebels against Bligh. This middle section is the best, even if the characters have been attenuated. Brando's Christian lacks Gable's unquestioning conviction and Howard's Bligh is not the sadistic psychopath Laughton played but an inflexible martinet who is aiming at a promotion. The issues are more finely textured, but the drama is thinner than in the 1935 version.

The third *Bounty*, with the Pitcairn Island segment, is atrocious. Christian helplessly watches his men sink into degradation and reasons with them to go back to England and plead their cause against Bligh. Brando is laden with lines like "Decency is worth dying for," so, presumably to stop him from pontificating everyone into a stupor, Richard Harris sets fire to the ship, where Brando is heroically charred while trying to save a companion. He has possibly the longest death scene in film history and certainly the most embarrassing.

Mutiny on the Bounty was a regrettable turning point in Brando's career. He was indicted as another member of the star-system conspiracy, then furiously on trial with Elizabeth Taylor's *Cleopatra*. Brando would not be pilloried, and he threatened to take MGM to court for dumping all the blame of the *Bounty* disaster on him. There must have been considerable truth in his claim, because the studio issued a quick retraction.

Brando sealed the peace treaty with MGM by attending the film's premiere in Denver and signing autographs like an obedient star on display. But nothing could help *Mutiny on the Bounty*, not even seven Academy Award nominations, including an unaccountable one for best film. The final shot of the picture was prophetic: the ship sinks in flames and so did the movie, brought down by a budget it could not possibly recoup.

Brando had adamantly refused any responsibility as captain, but he went down with the *Bounty* anyway. No one—least of all Brando—realized it, but his lean years were just around the corner.

MUTINY ON THE BOUNTY (1962). With Trevor Howard, Richard Harris, and Percy Herbert.

By 1962, box-office poison was an obsolete term, once applied to thirties and forties stars of waning power, but it was recoined for Brando after the accumulated loss of *The Fugitive Kind, One-Eyed Jacks,* and *Mutiny on the Bounty.* At last, like Booth Tarkington's young Amberson, the arrogant brat had gotten his come-uppance.

But Brando was no longer a brat. His post-*Bounty* films were rejected not because he was under a box-office curse, but because he had grown up as a man and as an actor. The erstwhile rebel dared to reverse his whole mystique and started playing figures of authority, maladjusted men in a different scale of society. The earthbound Peter Pan had lost his capacity for liberating flight; audiences and critics found it hard to forgive him.

With MacWhite, the U.S. ambassador in *The Ugly American,* Brando played his first born loser, the existential hero who fully realizes he is waging a futile fight against impossible odds. This was to be the pattern of his finest and most underrated performances in the sixties, from *The Chase* to *Reflections in a Golden Eye* to *Burn!* The fifties Brando had always given the impression of coming out on top, even in chastisement or heroic death. With *The Ugly American* the Brando character first hit rock bottom.

CHAPTER V

THE LEAN YEARS

The film also heralds a late Brando tendency to shuffle roles and play the part his antagonist held in a previous movie. Despite MacWhite's troubled dignity in *The Ugly American,* he is basically the same well-meaning, ineffectual, ingenuous American abroad that the Fords — Glenn and Paul — played in *The Teahouse of the August Moon,* while the Asian revolutionary Deong (Eiji Okada) is a disconcerting mixture of Sakini and Zapata.

The Ugly American takes place in the mythical country of Sarkhan, clearly a stand-in for Vietnam. The film starts with newly appointed Ambassador MacWhite seeking confirmation from the Senate Committee on Foreign Relations. Brando is at his fussy best as he faces suspicious and tricky interrogators while fumbling with his pipe and glasses, carefully checking arrogance and squelching anger with a calculated boyishness.

The main reason for sending MacWhite to Sarkhan is that he knows the country, having parachuted into it for intelligence work during World War II. He had also been a guerrilla comrade and personal friend of Deong, now the much respected — and dreaded —

THE UGLY AMERICAN (1963).
As Harrison Carter MacWhite.

convivial reunion that Brando plays to comic perfection as he tries to woo the Sarkhanese back into his friendly orbit. It is a shrewd portrait of the nice American trying— maybe too hard—to be liked on foreign soil: when offered an exotic delicacy, Brando radiates the joy of recognition by murmuring, "It's a kosher pickle."

The honeymoon with Deong is brief, and their friendship gets sourer and spicier than the pickle. So does the film. Deong begins to spout one dog-eared Communist slogan after another. Fighting his rudimentary English, Eiji Okada's confused political jargon becomes unintelligible, as he circles around Brando, stomping the floor and flailing his arms like a demented marionette. This very essential scene of ideological contradictions is uncomfortably similar to the clashes between Yul Brynner and Deborah Kerr in *The King and I*, up to a fatal point where Okada seems about to sing "Shall we dance?"

The picture never recovers from this lapse, though Brando movingly conveys the anguish of a man faced with nonexistent choices. He calls Deong a Judas goat, and Deong counters by labeling MacWhite a Yankee imperialist. The ambassador escalates the insults by branding Deong a full-fledged Communist. As it turns out at the end, Deong was merely a "Com-

leader of the opposition to the puppet regime shored by the United States. At the airport, minutes after his arrival, MacWhite's car is attacked and almost overturned by an angry mob of anti-American demonstrators. He arrives at the embassy in barely controlled rage at his incompetent, golf-playing staff. Brando does not raise his voice and yet each word is a shout as he icily tells them: "I was afraid out there, but I did not know what fear was until I got to this meeting."

MacWhite and Deong renew their old acquaintance in a boozy,

THE UGLY AMERICAN (1963). With Arthur Hill and Frances Helm.

THE UGLY AMERICAN (1963). With Eiji Okada.

THE UGLY AMERICAN (1963). With Pat Hingle, Sandra Church, and Judson Pratt.

munist dupe," quickly eliminated by the Party as soon as he stops serving their purposes. But all the name-calling and fine semantic distinctions are tragically pointless while Sarkhan is erupting into flaming civil war as Deong expires in MacWhite's helpless arms.

The film is uncannily prophetic of American involvement in Southeast Asia and so pessimistic that it refuses to come to life as drama.

The effective ending shows MacWhite's despairing last stand at a press conference relayed to a home television set in middle America. Blandly watching the impassioned speech, a bored man clicks off Brando's pleas into oblivion. It is a sadly appropriate conclusion to a film that had painted itself into a dark, inescapable corner. Brando's performance does not save *The Ugly American* from being grim but unenlightening, a tragedy without a catharsis.

George Englund and Stewart Stern, director and writer of *The Ugly American*, dreamed up another story about Southeast Asia for Brando, who had become fascinated by the region. *A Tiger by the Tail* was to be co-produced by Pennebaker Productions and the United Nations. It told about a parasitical "society doctor" who gets tired of his rich wife and hypochondriacal patients. He goes to work for WHO, the World Health Organization, somewhere in Asia, and lives romantically with a native girl who bears him a child and then dies in a cholera epidemic. This is as far as the project went, for the UN shied away from the film, apparently because it was felt that WHO would never recruit that type of doctor. The lofty, idealistic film (half *The Citadel*, half *The Rains Came*) was never made, and Pennebaker was sold for one million dollars to MCA-Universal where Brando made *Bedtime Story* instead.

This 1964 film is usually given short shrift but is one of Brando's most revealing, a curious black comedy in which the star reaches a crossroads, elects self-immolation, and seems to be saying good-bye to all the roles he was acclaimed for at one point or another in his career. The screenplay is by Stanley Shapiro, at that time Universal's Oscar-winning writer of the highly marketable Doris Day-Rock Hudson comedies. On the strength of their box-office popularity Shapiro gained producer status, and his script, written in collaboration with Paul Henning, lets all the underlying nasty humor bubble to the surface in *Bedtime Story*.

The film is Billy Wilder without the German rigor or Ernst Lubitsch without the Berliner charm. As directed by Ralph Levy, it is as American as apple pie— with a worm in every bite. Brando plays Benson, a Casanova who despises women and invents all sorts of tricks to bed them and leave them. His favorite one is going through Germany posing as an American GI of Teutonic extraction. Whenever he spots a girl he likes, he takes a Polaroid picture of her house, knocks on the door waving the photo and pretending to be on a pilgrimage to this very cottage his grandmother so vividly described. It is an infallible system for a hit-and-run seduction.

Benson seems content with this game until he meets Jamison (David Niven), a real operator who has learned to combine sex with money. Jamison poses as an exiled prince and not only gets women to share his bed but also to bestow their jewels on him for the sake of the counterrevolution. Benson-

BEDTIME STORY (1964). With Susanne Cramer.

Brando decides to corner Jamison-Niven's market on sex plus finance. A contest develops, and whoever wins will dominate a small Riviera resort as "King of the Mountain," the film's original title.

In *Bedtime Story* Brando blithely, suicidally disfigures his gallery of film portraits. In his early seductions of sentimental *Maedchen* he resurrects the Christian Diestl stance from *The Young Lions,* from the jutting chin to the slightly guttural accent. Then, in a train compartment where he meets Niven, he becomes a comic Kowalski as he expounds his woman-hating credo, smashing his fist into his hand to demonstrate how females must be crushed.

Brando blackmails Niven into a reluctant partnership, then assumes the role of Albuino, the fake prince's insane brother who conveniently scares matrons away after they have been swindled. He combs his hair down as in *Julius Caesar* and dons a Napoleonic uniform out of *Desirée.* He growls, scowls, babbles, and dribbles, a monstrous mutation of past idols, underlining the implicit megalomania in Antony and Bonaparte, now run full course into madness.

In this Brando revue of self-parody, the strangest turn comes last. In the competition with Niven both men have set themselves the goal of cheating the American Soap Queen (Shirley Jones), and Brando's trick is unbeatable. He gets into a wheelchair, pretends to be a paraplegic veteran, and mercilessly plays on the girl's sympathy. *The Men,* that landmark film, is further desecrated in a macabrely funny scene where Niven, posing as a doctor, whips the paraplegic's supposedly desensitized legs while Brando sobbingly holds back each scream, in a take-off of the frequent beatings he had received in his film career.

Audiences watched the sacrilege in shock. Critic Dwight Mac-Donald even suggested that some sadist might eventually concoct a double bill of *The Men* and *Bedtime Story* at a hospital for paralyzed veterans. Brando had wiped his slate clean, but it was an empty gesture. He came back to the screen soon enough with *Morituri* (1965).

Morituri could have been a good film. It was based on a novel by Werner Joerg Luedecke, an assistant naval attaché in Tokyo, who

BEDTIME STORY (1964). With Shirley Jones and David Niven.

BEDTIME STORY (1964). With David Niven.

was sent back to Germany as a prisoner in a blockade runner when the Nazis discovered he was part Jewish. The film tells a parallel story about a rich, anti-Nazi German in India (Brando) who is persuaded by a British agent (Trevor Howard) to board a German blockade runner en route from Japan to Occupied France in 1942. Sabotage is to be his undercover mission.

As Robert Crain, Brando again plays Christian Diestl: cropped hair, dilatory speech, and a German accent so thick that he actually says "very interesting" just like Arte Johnson, who later turned the line into a ludicrous catch-phrase on the television show "Laugh-In." Brando and co-star Yul Brynner

appear to be in different films altogether; Brynner's is an action melodrama and Brando's is the moral parable of a disenchanted man who cannot stop fighting evil, not out of any lasting conviction but almost as a physical reflex. Only at the very end of the film do both images come to any meaningful contact, as Brynner asks Brando: "If you have nothing to believe in, why did you blow up the ship?" and Brando grumbles: "It doesn't matter now."

His last line defines the purpose of the character and the film, but it came so late that it more accurately echoes Brando's disappointment with the paltry results of this promising project. Much of the blame

THE SABOTEUR · CODE NAME MORITURI (1965) As Robert Crain

THE SABOTEUR: CODE NAME MORITURI (1965). With Yul Brynner.

belongs to Swiss director Bernhard Wicki who, after considerable European success with *The Bridge*, was transplanted to Hollywood and rapidly withered on the vine. In 1964 he directed an unfortunate adaptation of Friedrich Dürrenmatt's *The Visit* with a miscast Ingrid Bergman and a misguided Anthony Quinn. *Morituri* was his second film in America, and Wicki was unable to meld the disparate styles of Brando, Brynner, and Howard. The result was an abortive, lukewarm thriller, bogged in the pseudo-profundities of Daniel Taradash's screenplay.

Commercially and artistically, *Morituri* was stillborn. After its first few weeks in release the title was changed to *Code Name: Morituri* and finally to *The Saboteur: Code Name Morituri*. Words multiplied on the marquee but could not add revenue to an appalling flop. To

help the moribund *Morituri*, Brando agreed to participate in a marathon, day-long series of filmed interviews with reporters from local TV stations across the country.

This mind-boggling event took place at the Hotel Vanderbilt in New York and was recorded on film by the Maysles brothers. The end result is *Meet Marlon Brando*, one of the star's least known films. In this 29-minute documentary Brando plays himself as master of the put-down and prince of biting sarcasm. One after another, interviewers are brought to his presence like frightened Christians to be devoured by an imperious lion. He mocks, jeers, and sneers at them with inexhaustible glee.

He flirts outrageously with a luscious blonde reporter who is haltingly trying to find something relevant to ask him as he stops her in mid-sentence by whispering: "Excuse me for touching your ankle." Another woman politely says, "You're not an ugly American," and he retorts: "When did you last see me in the nude?" Embarrassed, she rushes to say something flattering and congratulates him on *Morituri*. When it turns out she had not yet seen the movie, he lectures her sternly: "You must not believe propaganda. It might be terrible and you don't know." Looking for a bright exit line, the chastened lady gushes: "This is your whole personality in a capsule." He paralyzes her with: "And how do you know what my personality is?"

It is hard to believe that all the interviews were conducted on this vitriolic level, and such *cinema verité* features as *Salesman* and *Gimme Shelter* later proved the Maysles brothers' allegiance to the school of revelation by indiscretion, wherein someone is thought to be more vividly revealed when caught picking his nose. In *Meet Marlon Brando* the star is obviously irked by the foolish barrage of questioning, but it is difficult for a man to sustain an attitude of intellectual and moral superiority when he is beamingly declaring: "I'm a huckster and I'm here thumping the tub for *Morituri*."

In Hollywood *Morituri* certified

Brando's decline, yet Sam Spiegel, his producer in *On the Waterfront*, was still one of the faithful. He had initially thought of Brando for *Lawrence of Arabia* before it was decided that the role needed a new face: Peter O'Toole. The game of star permutation came full circle when Brando took O'Toole's role in Spiegel's *The Chase* (1966). O'Toole felt he would look ridiculous as a Texas sheriff and risked being sued by Spiegel to escape the film. He must also have read the incoherent screenplay that Brando accepted, again after promised revisions that never reached the screen. Lillian Hellman wrote and Arthur Penn directed the picture; of Brando's sixties reversals from rebel to figure of authority, *The Chase* marks the almost perfect about-face.

Val Rogers (E. G. Marshall), the all-powerful tycoon, has appointed Calder (Brando) as sheriff of a small Southern town, hinting that he can only go so far and must never jeopardize Rogers's crooked interests. Sheriff Calder is the exact equivalent of the part Robert Keith played as *The Wild One's* weak antagonist, but Brando invests it with the rigid bearing of a man of honor caught in a dishonorable dilemma.

The part is skeletal, but he fleshes it out with a fine performance. Director Penn had envi-

THE CHASE (1966). As Sheriff Calder.

THE CHASE (1966). With Angie Dickinson.

sioned Calder as an existential hero who stubbornly upholds sanity in a community gone crazy. The text, in Penn's own words, was "stilted and excessively expository," so he asked Brando to improvise. "He did it brilliantly," Penn has said. "It was inarticulate and raw, but passionate." All of these scenes disappeared in the final cut, and Penn calls them "a great loss of some of the best acting I'd ever witnessed."

What remains of *The Chase* is a sort of Don Quixote rewritten by Sartre, as Calder is placed for one night in a desperate situation. Bubber Reeves (Robert Redford), the town rebel, has escaped from a chain gang and is moving closer to town. His wife (Jane Fonda) has been carrying on with Val Rogers's son (James Fox), and Rogers knows Bubber has to be killed before he learns the truth and becomes a threat to his boy.

Sheriff Calder is pressured to locate Bubber as soon as possible, but he knows that finding him is tantamount to becoming a finger man for Rogers's henchmen. In Brando's acting *The Chase* reverberates with echoes of classic film portraits of knights in shining armor against rampant corruption. He confronts tycoon Marshall much as James Stewart faced Edward Arnold in *Mr. Smith Goes to Washington* and then suffers the town's indifference with a stoicism eminiscent of Gary Cooper in *High Noon*. But this is not the rainbow-edged world of Capra's fables, nor does it have the puritan ethics of Zinnemann's. *The Chase* happens in the dark, menacing South of Lillian Hellman's nightmares, and in this work her nihilism is redolent of hysteria. Arthur Penn emphasizes the frenzy, and *The Chase* is often as unbelievable —and as funny—as *Walpurgisnacht* staged by the Marx brothers.

Brando was fortunate to have a part that kept him at the edge of the vortex, but his work has to be extracted from the barrel of rotten apples *The Chase* becomes. If Penn had been able to expand Brando's part and focus on it, the film would have had the strength of his good scenes, like the one in which even the convict's mother (Miriam Hopkins) offers the sheriff her savings to let Bubber get away. "Shut up, you goddamned woman!" Brando explodes, but then his rage subsides as he sighs dejectedly, "What did I do to make all these people think they could buy me?"

Here is the real core of *The Chase*, but as the screenplay stands, Calder's plight becomes a mere subplot, a solid lower story to

THE CHASE (1966).
With Miriam Hopkins.

THE CHASE (1966). With
Robert Redford.

113

THE CHASE (1966). On the set with sister Jocelyn.

a tottering tower of Babel. In the bizarre climax Redford is shot, Brando is pummeled, and Fox is crushed, as teenagers chant, fireworks flare, and Martha Hyer munches on her pearl necklace. At a memorably raucous first preview, the entire audience, including critics, laughed its head off.

Failure is fatherless, and Penn explained that the film had been ruinously edited in London, behind his back. Miss Hellman claimed her original screenplay had been destroyed by Penn, Spiegel, and a writer they hired. Disowned by one and all, *The Chase* had an inglorious commercial career.

In the mid-sixties Brando had divorced Movita and was fighting steep alimony payments in a protracted legal hassle. He had bought an island in Tahiti where he lived between film assignments with Tarita, his co-star of *Mutiny on the Bounty,* and their son Tehotu. The legal entanglements with Ann Kashfi were far from unraveled. Financial pressures seem the only clue to his accepting *The Appaloosa* (1966), an ordinary Western.

Brando plays a buffalo hunter who abandons his trade to start his own cattle ranch, breeding mares to his Appaloosa stallion. A bad hombre (John Saxon) steals the horse, and in typical sex revenge his woman runs away with Brando. The film is an empty recapitulation of past themes, including the almost ritualistic punishment Brando endured in so many films, this time in a scene where he is tied to a rampaging horse.

Director Sidney J. Furie, whose spy melodrama *The Ipcress File* had been a popular success, burdened *The Appaloosa* with similar zoom shots, trick editing, and tortured angles, but this elementary plot had no sinews to support them. When Brando balked at following the illogical screenplay, Furie accused him of loving chaos. Brando clearly lost interest and underacts to the point of absenteeism; the film is dominated by Saxon's amusingly hammy villain. Some critics wrote that Brando had

THE APPALOOSA (1966). As Matt.

THE APPALOOSA (1966). With John Saxon.

THE APPALOOSA (1966). With Anjanette Comer.

handed Saxon the film on a silver platter, but considering the quality of *The Appaloosa*, it was more in a tin bucket.

Brando's star was dimming, but it was never more lackluster than in the ill-fated *A Countess from Hong Kong* (1967). After long retirement in Switzerland, Charles Chaplin announced he had a new screenplay ready for filming. In this anemic comedy a destitute exiled Russian countess has resorted to prostitution in Hong Kong and must escape the police by boarding a ship as a stowaway. She hides in the cabin of an American millionaire, newly appointed ambassador to Saudi Arabia. After many an embarrassing situation he falls in love with her and leaves his stuffy wife to redeem the beautiful sinner.

To insure himself a strong marquee lure, producer Jerome Epstein signed Brando and Sophia Loren for the leads. *A Countess from Hong Kong* became a modern version of "The Emperor's New Clothes," with no one daring to shout the truth: the screenplay was awful. The miracles Chaplin was expected to perform on the set were not forthcoming. He laughed uproariously at his own jokes, and the players went through the motions, pretending fresh farce could be squeezed from the stale situations.

*A COUNTESS
FROM HONG KONG (1967).
With Sophia Loren.*

Publicity shots of the filming show Chaplin miming every gesture for his stars to copy. Nothing could have been worse for Brando, who needs the breathing space of spontaneity. With another director he probably would have walked off the set, but out of deference for the grand old man he became Chaplin's puppet, in a performance so mechanical one can almost hear his sinews crack during the worst slapstick or his molars grind between lines like "This is the first real happiness I've ever known" or "I wonder what your fate would have been had you been in similar circumstances."

Brando played a capitalist stuffed-shirt, exactly the sort of character destined to be demolished in a film by Chaplin, whose sense of comedy often hinges on loss of dignity and lofty callings interrupted by the call of nature. Brando, as the inflexible ambassador, is the butt of many a feeble joke, and the film abounds in trouser-dropping, bathroom humor, and seasick characters in search of available portholes. Brando wades through it all with grim determination, as if he were enacting the tribulations of Job for the Moscow Art Theatre. It is impossible to separate the character's humiliation from the actor's.

This unpleasant experience was fortunately followed by Brando's best picture in the lean sixties: *Reflections in a Golden Eye* (1967). The film version of Carson McCullers's novella had been planned for Montgomery Clift, and after the actor's death in 1966 Brando took the role. Clift would have been perhaps too vulnerable and frail, but the part seemed so deceptively ideal for him that many voiced doubts that Brando could play it.

A COUNTESS FROM HONG KONG (1967). With Sophia Loren.

REFLECTIONS IN A GOLDEN EYE (1967). With Elizabeth Taylor.

ohn Huston, a tough, logical irector, was also considered the rong choice for this convoluted le of spiraling perversion and outhern discomfort.

Yet the Brando-Huston combi-ation gave the film a gravity, a eserve, a stillness at the center; e flamboyant material is dealt ith in a precise equivalent of IcCullers's spartan prose. The :ladys Hall-Chapman Mortimer creenplay follows the slender book uithfully: it is the story of a major n a Southern Army post who, after ears of admiring the orderliness of nilitary life and the manly camara-lerie of the barracks, comes to ealize his feelings are masks for a atent homosexuality.

His sluttish wife Leonora (Eliza-beth Taylor) has channeled her sex-ual frustration into an affair with their next-door neighbor, Colonel Langdon (Brian Keith), and Mrs. Langdon (Julie Harris) expresses her dejection by slashing off her nipples with garden shears. Mean-while, Major Penderton has fallen hopelessly in love with an almost catatonically withdrawn soldier (Robert Forster) who—in turn obsessed with Leonora—watches her from afar with the isolated pas-sion of the voyeur.

The inherent hysteria in these interlocking triangles is reined by Huston and his gifted cast, espe-cially Brando. As Major Penderton he holds himself carefully erect, like a marble statue that senses its own cracking down the middle and fears crumbling at any false move. He wears his own flesh like a stifling garment he would gladly discard. Brando had put on weight for the role, and he is heartbreakingly pathetic as he bobs around on a horse, in grotesque imitation of the lithe beauty he admires in the young soldier. Yet there is the narcissism of the daily workout, as he keeps his middle-aged body taut, in a last ditch attempt at desirability, waiting for the final date that will never come.

The performance is minutely studied yet magically spontaneous. There is the total concentration of the truly mad as Penderton fails to respond to the sound of a car crashing behind his back and keeps on following the private, oblivious of the people running past him to the scene of the accident. As if all the reservoir of "sense memory" classes had come back to him from his Method days, he is revealing in his relation to objects, as he lovingly caresses a candy wrapper the soldier left behind and hides it like a treasured love memento in a box, along with his secret photographs of naked statues, a stolen silver spoon, and other monsters from an unconfessable Id.

His great aria comes when he starts lecturing his military students on the qualities of leader-

ship, realizes his own inadequac[y] and stifles a racking sob in front [of] the class. The last ten minutes [of] *Reflections in a Golden Eye* ar[e] pantomime and contain nearly th[e] best acting in Brando's career. Th[e] soldier has sneaked into the hous[e] to watch Leonora sleep, and Pe[n]derton, in his madness, thinks th[at] is at last the longed-for arrival of h[is] gentleman caller. With pitif[ul] coquetry he fixes two strands [of] hair over his balding forehead an[d] sits waiting, until he discovers th[e] man is in his wife's bedroom. Pen[-]derton has been jilted and cuck[-]olded at the same time.

He silently stares at Leonora['s] door, and then Huston does some[-]thing a director can attempt onl[y] with an actor like Marlon Brand[o]. The camera focuses on the doo[r] and the actor moves away. Fo[r] about half a minute he is not ther[e] but the cumulative force of his per[-]sonality fills the empty frame. Th[e] audience identifies with Pender[-]ton's torment and follows him i[n] spirit, anticipating his return wit[h] dread, because he must surel[y] come back with a murderous gun.

Brando kills the interloper, no[t] as a jealous husband but as [a] rejected suitor. In the last master[-]ful shot the camera careens i[n] frenetic pans from the dead body t[o] the screaming Taylor and t[o] Brando, who rubs his finger[s] against the bridge of his nose

REFLECTIONS IN A GOLDEN EYE (1967). With Elizabeth Taylor and Robert Forster.

suggesting how Penderton has taken off the distorting glasses of insane love and now must readjust his vision to the horror around him, reversing the patterns of sleep to wake up in a nightmare.

To suit Miss Taylor's wishes, the Southern saturnalia of *Reflections in a Golden Eye* had been filmed in Rome, and Brando stayed in Europe for a couple of films. *The Night of the Following Day*, held back for release until 1968, is such a peculiar, hermetically sealed thriller that the main mystery is what the parties involved had in mind while creating it.

The director, Hubert Cornfield, was a man of perennially unjelled promise who had built himself a demi-cult with several failed but interesting films: *Plunder Road*, *Pressure Point*, and *The Third Voice*. He had acquired film rights to *The Snatchers*, a novel by Leonard White whose *Clean Break* had been made into Stanley Kubrick's 1956 "sleeper," *The Killing* and whose *Obsession* had been turned upside down by Jean-Luc Godard in *Pierrot le Fou* (1965).

The plot has a teenage heiress (Pamela Franklin) picked up at Orly airport by her father's chauffeur (Brando), who takes her to a remote beach house on the coast of Normandy. Chauffeur—no other name is given for the enigmatic character—is in league with kid-

THE NIGHT OF THE FOLLOWING DAY (1968). As the Chauffeur.

nappers: Leer (Richard Boone), sadistic killer; Vi (Rita Moreno), cocaine addict; and her brother Wally (Jess Hahn), a moronic thug.

Chauffeur is revolted by Leer's sadism and attracted by his nubile captive. He fights to the death with Leer in the sand dunes and, as sole survivor of the gang, returns to the house to find the girl brutally tortured and either dead or unconscious. It does not matter which, for she opens her eyes to find herself again on the same plane she arrived on, with Chauffeur Brando waiting for her, like a uniformed angel of death out of Jean Cocteau

circular film falls between
ntmare, hallucination, and pre-
nition. And also between bland
n chowder and overspiced
illabaise.

like a belated surfer riding the
splash of the waning French
ν Wave, Cornfield had tried to
isform a tough, American-type
nap thriller into a stylized,
amlike French-style film á la
dard-Truffaut. The decor is
inously bare; the dialogue
ıly poetic or zombielike; the sit-
ions so disjointed it is anybody's
ıss whether they are meant to be
comic or are just unintentionally
laughable.

In a film so blank and impenetra-
ble anything goes, and Brando
launched another full repertory of
past impersonations. Thin to ema-
ciation, he is blonder than his German demi-god in *The Young Lions*,
and he erupts with the tongue-tied
venom of *The Wild One. The Night
of the Following Day* is the kind of
cinema double crostic that always
finds its partisans, but general
audiences hate to be perplexed and
teased. Even in its meager dis-
tribution it was an open-and-shut

THE NIGHT OF THE FOLLOWING DAY (1968). With Jess Hahn.

THE NIGHT OF THE FOLLOWING DAY
(1968). With Pamela Franklin.

se almost within days of its
layed release.

In November 1967, Christian
arquand, one of Brando's long-
me friends, sought his coopera-
n on a film version of *Candy*, a
rry Southern-Mason Hoffenberg
vel that parlayed soft-core por-
graphy and clever style into a
andalous success. Brando was
strumental in lining up Richard
rton for the cast. With these two
ars as guarantee, the project
tracted financing, as well as sev-
al other celebrities for its cast.

Under Marquand's flashy-flabby
rection *Candy* degenerated into a
ries of star turns with Brando,
irton, James Coburn, Walter

CANDY (1968). With Ewa Aulin.

Matthau, John Huston, Charles
Aznavour, and Ringo Starr as the
libidinous men that *Candy*, the

CANDY (1968). With Ewa Aulin.

sexual Candide, finds in her optimistic trail to innocent corruption. Brando's sketch was the last, a mistake in timing. At the tail end of this addled movie even the most mindless moviegoer was ready to give up and leave.

The law of diminishing returns blights a performance that is quite funny when taken out of context. Brando plays a Guru who switches mannerisms and accents so dizzyingly that he sounds like Barbra Streisand in one shot and like Peter Sellers's Pakistani imitation in the next. His opening moment is priceless, as he tries to unscramble himself from the Yoga lotus position, letting all petals fall where they may.

His caricature of the standard Brando monologue is ruthless, as he tells Candy that her name is cabalistic, a five-letter pentagram ending in Y, the symbol of the Yoni. As the verbal seduction proceeds full steam, he fiddles with his hair like a demented female impersonator and minces around his pond, flinging a wet toga like Tiny Tim auditioning for Marc Antony.

When Candy learns he can converse with vegetables, she is mesmerized, and the Guru beds her and beds her in a tangle of sheets, limbs, and conflicting manes—his black and greasy, hers flaxen and flaccid. Buck Henry's screenplay made the Brando sketch into a

take-off of *Lolita's* cross-count[ry] motel-to-motel movable sex fea[ture.] Candy and the Guru travel ti[re]lessly in a refrigerator truck t[hat] holds an Indian temple in its s[o] realistic bowels. Finally it starts [to] snow inside the truck, and Bran[do] shrivels in an avalanche as th[ey] cross still another state lin[e.] Turned into a glistening stalagmi[te,] he is found by two cops who deli[ver] the punch-line: "You can't brin[g a] frozen Guru into California."

When finally released, arou[nd] Christmas, 1968, *Candy* attract[ed] the curious, but it was never we[ll] liked. The stars seemed to be ha[v]ing so much fun making the fi[lm] that viewers felt the resentment [of] watching a neighbor throw a wi[ld] party to which they had not be[en] invited.

Back in America after his Eur[o]pean jaunt, Brando was preparin[g,] in the spring of 1968, for wh[at] Hollywood considered his do-o[r-] die film. *Candy* and *The Night [of] the Following Day* had yet to me[et] their sour reception, but *Refle[c]tions in a Golden Eye* had been [a] critical and financial disappoin[t]ment. Producers were convince[d] that Brando could only work we[ll] with Elia Kazan, and the star wa[s] called upon to confirm or deny th[is] unfounded judgment with *Th[e] Arrangement*.

Kazan's novel centered around [a] writer who had sold out to the com[-]

BURN! (1970).
As Sir William Walker.

"The part made him uncomfortable," Kazan said. "It was very, very close to something basic in him." Yet whatever Brando's motives for walking out on *The Arrangement*, his decision was sound. The film, starring Kirk Douglas, is Kazan's worst. And Brando underlined his intention of playing only socially significant roles by rejecting a potential hit like *Butch Cassidy and the Sundance Kid* to go into *Quemada*, later known as *Queimada* and finally as *Burn!* (1970).

Burn! is the ultimate reversal of the Brando image, for the revolutionary becomes counterrevolutionary, and Brando's role is oddly similar to the treacherous camp follower Joseph Wiseman played in *Viva Zapata!* Sir William Walker is also the nearest thing to total villainy in the Brando canon: a man possessed by diabolic cynicism.

Walker comes to Queimada, a Portuguese island colony in the Caribbean in mid-1800s, as a British *agent provocateur*. He invents a native hero in José Dolores (Evaristo Márquez) and manipulates him into triumphant revolution. José Dolores ascends the governor's throne and begins to take himself too seriously as leader of a black-ruled republic. This goes against Walker's plans of opening the sugar trade to the British market. Walker convinces José Dolores

mercialism of the advertising business. The book had autobiographical overtones, and Kazan thought of Brando not only as the best actor he had ever worked with but also as a quasi-surrogate and movie alter ego. Then, in April of 1968, Martin Luther King was assassinated, and Brando abandoned the Kazan project, declaring he would devote himself to work in the civil rights movement.

In an interview in *Movie* magazine Kazan suggests that Brando was afraid of the similarity between the protagonist of *The Arrangement* and Brando's own image as an artist who had failed his initial promise.

BURN! (1970). With Renato Salvatori.

that he cannot maintain civilization on the island without active white support. Fearing the hazards of no commerce or contact with the outside world, José Dolores lays down his arms, and Walker departs, his mission accomplished.

Ten years later the film finds him in London, utterly dishonored and bitter. He has been cashiered by the admiralty and is now a brawling, drunken wreck. Yet he is the only man who knows Queimada, so the Royal Sugar Company dredges him up from a sleazy bar and returns him to the island, newly troubled by José Dolores's revolutionary comeback.

With paranoid zeal, Walker prepares himself to destroy his own creation. He sets a torch to half the island to smoke out the guerillas, and *Burn!* becomes a political horror film; the evil doctor cannot control his cleverly indoctrinated monster and tries to destroy him by fire. Immortality must be denied to José Dolores at all costs. "A hero becomes a martyr and then a myth," Walker says. "Songs will go through the Antilles about him, and Royal Sugar controls many islands." "Better songs than armies," a cautious officer reminds him. "Better silence than songs," Walker insists.

After capturing José Dolores, Walker argues with him, trying to justify his own position, but the rebel spits in his face. Morally beaten, Walker even cuts the captive's ropes on the night before the execution, but José Dolores refuses to escape and mocks him with his saintliness. The black man dies heroically, and Walker is ignominiously stabbed by one of his partisans, in an ending that underscores the Christ-Judas dichotomy that runs through the film.

Brando's performance is multilayered as he sways from compulsive destructiveness to suffocating regret. Walker despises himself but cannot stop, because only the annihilation of José Dolores gives some meaning to his wretched life. As Franco Solinas and Giorgio Arlorio wrote it, *Burn!* is a Marxist allegory that aspires to liberating fervor and sometimes descends into clanking rhetoric, yet Brando turns it into quasi-Shakespearean tragedy of honor lost and dignity retained.

The filming was, once again, stormy. Brando admired director Gillo Pontecorvo's classic revolutionary film, *The Battle of Algiers*, but both men disagreed frequently on the set. "I really would like to kill him," Brando told *Life* magazine. *Burn!* started abortively in Colombia, moved to North Africa, and was concluded in sound stages in Rome's Cinecitta. It is a powerful film, but its flashes of greatness are never integrated into a whole.

THE NIGHTCOMERS (1972). As Quint.

Middling reviews condemned it to quick death in the art circuit.

Brando was inactive for a while, resting in Tahiti with Tarita, his son, and a new daughter, named after her mother. He went back to England for *The Nightcomers* (1972), which could be subtitled "Events Leading to the Turn of the Screw." The Michael Hastings screenplay follows Flora and Miles, the bedeviled children of Henry James's novel, at the time they fall under the influence of Quint and Miss Jessel, the gardener and governess who would later loom over them as ghostly presences. In Hastings's fanciful interpretation the children ape the troubled sex life of the couple and eventually kill them.

Brando plays Quint as a primitive brute who innocently corrupts Flora and Miles with his distorted credo: hate is love, death is life, and "If you love somebody you really want to kill them." He is sweet, tender, delightfully avuncular, as he unwittingly poisons their minds. He paints on mustaches, makes funny faces, and in a thick Irish brogue tells them the story of how his father swindled a gypsy by selling him a dolled-up nag. It is one of Brando's better monologues, and the laughter congeals as he suddenly reviews the transparently false tale and grumbles, "That was my father."

With Miss Jessel (Stephanie Beacham) he has a relationship that heightens all of his previous characters' traumas. Sex is again the social equalizer between the gardener and the haughty governess, a Siamese twin composed of both Blanche and Stella DuBois. Night after night they enact a sadomasochistic charade in which he ties her to the bedposts, lashes her, and then mock-rapes her. The infinitely sad thing is that Quint is playing the part Miss Jessel forces on him, and the film's climax hinges on this revelation.

The children convince Quint that Miss Jessel really loves him

THE NIGHTCOMERS (1972). With Thora Hird.

THE NIGHTCOMERS (1972). With Stephanie Beacham.

and play Cupid for a romantic tryst. Quint-Brando combs his scraggly mane and perfumes his hairy chest, but Miss Jessel bitchily tells him he looks uncomfortable. He is turned off by her panting desire for submission and pain but still tries to save the last shreds of their twisted love as he kisses her delicately and begs her: "I need you to stay with me." "In your pigsty?" she coldly answers. "I'll give you pigsty," he yells as he savagely punches her, knowing now that he has only been feeding her hunger for abasement.

It is a good part and a penetrating performance in a film unworthy of either. Michael Winner directed *The Nightcomers* with his usual empty flourishes. The chopped editing confuses the narrative and the restless zoom lenses add to the disorientation. Bad reviews and worse box-office could have driven the last nails through Brando's dead-star coffin, but by the time *The Nightcomers* opened, early in 1972, it did not matter. This film was the past, and he was already into the future: *The Godfather* had rebaptized him.

Analyzing his rise and fall as a movie star, Brando told *Oui* magazine: "People pay money to have someone else act out their fantasies. It's like having a household pet: you endow the animal with qualities it might not have. It is the same with an actor: you have one or two emotional experiences with him and you begin to trust him. He becomes your favorite fantasy-maker. But when his performances contradict your feelings or oppose your way of life, then it's a lousy picture."

It is an accurate interpretation of the star syndrome—up to a point—because in Hollywood every cloud must have a silver lining and every tragedy aspires to a happy ending. Through the ages, saints and heroes went into the desert for meditation or around the world on perilous journeys or herculean tasks. In the twentieth century the stars, these last remnants of the ancient myths, are often forced into exile or plunged into decline until it is time for them to be newly acclaimed, in the ritual known as the "come-back."

For an actor of Brando's dramatic stature and social influence nothing short of an apotheosis would do. And after nearly twenty years of disappointment and rejection he came back in *The Godfather*, a film safely on its way to becoming the highest grosser in box-office histo-

THE GODFATHER AND TANGO

ry. It reinstated Brando upon the throne he had all but abdicated. But restoration, as usual, was not easy; it involved the intrigues of partisans, the opposition of miscreants, the arbitrariness of timing, the fickleness of luck.

Mario Puzo claims a redoubtable casting coup when he insists he wrote *The Godfather* with Brando in mind. It was a flash of author's intuition that failed to impress anyone else. When Paramount bought the novel, still in galley form, many names were initially shuffled for the part of Don Vito Corleone, including Anthony Quinn, Ernest Borgnine, Richard Conte, and even Carlo Ponti, Sophia Loren's producer-husband. After Francis Ford Coppola was assigned to direct the film, he was intrigued by Puzo's original idea and he called Brando. The actor desperately needed a popular success but was wary of still another Mafia story, so soon after Kirk Douglas's *The Brotherhood* had been indifferently received by critics and audiences.

Coppola insisted, and Brando, who swore he had never read a novel in his whole life, looked over a first treatment of the screenplay and then dipped into the pages of the runaway best seller to get an impression of Don Corleone. He liked the role enough to submit to what practically every star would have considered a crushing humiliation: he agreed to test for the part. The result is one of the most seductive legends in a legendary career. Brando himself conceived the rudimentary make-up; he plastered back his hair with grease, lined his cheeks and forehead with boot polish, and stuffed Kleenex around his gums. Over a steaming cup of coffee he moved his prestidigitator's fingers and mumbled a few words.

Coppola brought the homemade test to the studio and ran it for a diffident high echelon. "Sure he looks Italian," they said defensively, "but can he act?" When they learned it was actually Marlon Brando, a thrill of belated recognition electrified the meeting. Brando won the part but not the entire confidence of the studio. Too many flops weighed heavily on his star ledger; too many stories of past conflicts made him into a nearly unemployable sacred monster.

The Godfather was approached very tentatively as a film project. Coppola was given a stringent, penny-pinching budget. Brando began the movie at his most cooperative, sinking himself into the part in Stanislavskian identification, treating his screen children— Al Pacino, James Caan, Robert Duvall—as if they were his own, developing a paternalistic, prankish attitude with them. Jokingly, Brando was setting up the right atmosphere for an illusion of closely knit family life among the cast, but his lackadaisical behavior frightened the front office. Brando could or would not remember his lines, which he read from notes written on his shirt cuffs, in cards behind the camera, or on strategically placed bits of paper strewn around the props. The alarm was sounded, and the old misconceptions bubbled up. "Only Kazan can work with him" was inevitably the first. There was talk of firing Coppola and hiring Kazan, but Brando steadfastly stood by the young man who had faith in him, threatening to quit if Coppola was ousted.

Both stayed, of course, after the Italian wedding sequence was shot and edited to perfect timing and dramatic cadence. The studio was pleased and the budget considerably raised. *The Godfather* looked good enough to venture a few more millions on. The caution now seems excessive and the sums parsimonious when compared with the gold mine the film became, with a gross of over 100 million dollars in its first year in general release.

Even before its premiere critics

134

were gazing into their crystal balls to call it "the *Gone With The Wind* of gangster movies," but *The Godfather* turned out to be not only a box-office explosion but also a very fine film. With a quality that goes beyond style into cinematic alchemy, Coppola integrated the poetic vision of Visconti's *Rocco and his Brothers* with the jazzy dynamism of *Little Caesar*. The audience eavesdrops on these men who season spaghetti between murders, who keep their women pure while prostituting others, and who split themselves right down the middle into private friends and public enemies.

Everything in the film falls into place with a smooth precision that is never mechanical: the casting is inspired, the period recreation flawless, Coppola's control of the disparate elements unflagging. But *The Godfather* needs a godlike figure at its core. Brando gives it emotional roots: the good-bad, two-faced Janus of the early films now wears a cragged, eroded mask, but the everlasting ambivalence lurks in every wrinkle.

Brando's performance is a wonder of observation and understatement. He has the Italian accent and gestures down pat: the defiant-apologetic shrug, the hands that helplessly shoot up, the evanescent whiff of an "a" at the end of each noun. Yet he is neither

THE GODFATHER (1972).
As Don Corleone.

Vittorio de Sica nor Henry Armetta, for he found the essence at the bottom of the heady caricature. His cracked, dim voice suggests untold maladies, deeply inhaled Sicilian cigarettes, or the whirr of crushed coffee beans in an espresso machine. All the minute touches dovetail into the portrait of an aging monster, a tyrant grown benign.

From that first scene in which he lords it over his tawdry empire, dispensing vino and sympathy to

THE GODFATHER (1972). The Corleone wedding.

loosen a suppliant's tongue, Don Corleone is a figure for the audience to pity and fear. He is bored, like a doctor facing a roomful of hypochondriacs. After a series of petty requests, the beast in him flutters briefly to life when he orders the downfall of a Hollywood mogul in his now unforgettable line: "Make him an offer he can't refuse." Smelling a rose to clear the stench from his nostrils, he is then freed from dull care to go out into the sun and waltz, awkwardly elegant as a performing bear, with his newlywed daughter.

Brando brings to the film a deep political awareness. He plays Cor-

leone not as a sinister mobster but as an old tycoon whose line of business just happens to be crime. The problem of succession is foremost in his realm, and it makes the relationship between Don Vito and his youngest son, Michael (Al Pacino), all the more poignant. Pacino is excellent, improving as he is drawn into the Brando sphere which delineates and deepens his character; for example, in the hospital scene when Michael kisses the Don's hand, finally accepting him not as father but as godfather, with all the implications of the gesture in Mafia lore. Brando does not upstage Pacino but underlines the

young actor's performance wordlessly, as he rejects the obeisance
with a contracting mouth that sucks
in a regretful tear.

After his silent oath of allegiance
Michael is destined to follow the
family code. Thrown into the vendetta, he kills Don Corleone's enemies and goes into hiding in Sicily.
When he returns, his brother
Sonny is dead and Corleone's man-
tle is ready to be draped upon
Michael's no-longer-shrugging
shoulders. The old man's desire for
perpetuation is filled; he can then
peacefully descend into senility. As
Michael allots responsibility
between the remaining ranks,

Brando's Corleone tends to his
goldfish in a contented sag, his
spine happily relaxed, as if several
bones were missing but not sorely
missed.

Brando has never been afraid of
replaying scenes from his early suc-
cesses, as long as he could go
through the looking glass and
watch them from the opposite
viewpoint. His last memorable
conversation with Michael is a
reversal of the taxi scene in *On the
Waterfront*, with Brando now
assuming the Rod Steiger role as he
tells Michael: "I never wanted this
for you." His son could have had
class, he could have been a conten-

THE GODFATHER (1972).
With Al Pacino.

der, a Mafia figure in government a Governor or even President Corleone. Now his dream is tainted and family business must go on as usual.

Unafraid of traditional scene stealers, Brando plays his first scene with a cat, and he double dares by playing his last one with that actor's nemesis, a child. Director Coppola had welcomed and encouraged his suggestions, and Brando's gift for invention is at its highest as he distorts his mouth by pushing orange rinds over his gums to amuse his grandson with a trick that had always delighted the star's own children.

THE GODFATHER (1972). With Robert Duvall.

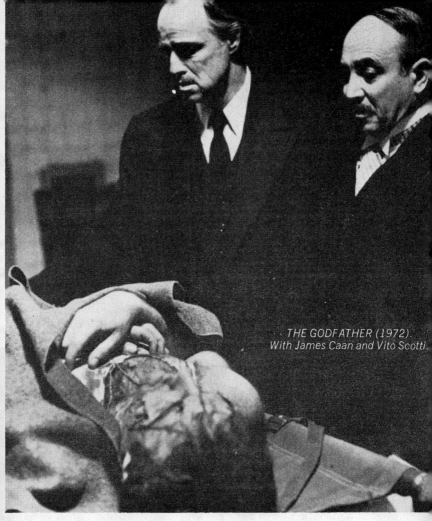

THE GODFATHER (1972).
With James Caan and Vito Scotti.

It is a pastoral interlude in an almost Sicilian leafy glade, but the improvised mask brings something sinister to it. Reviewers were quick to grasp the connection between this sequence and the one in *Frankenstein* where the monster menacingly plays with the child. Yet this time the monster is dying and the child survives. Corleone has difficulty sitting; he huffs and puffs before he grins malevolently through the artificial fangs. The child is frightened, but he is soon reassured it is his own grandfather.

No man is a monster to his own

kin, Brando's performance suggests, in a summation of the whole ethos of *The Godfather*. Enraptured with the game, Corleone pursues the child until he keels over, stricken like a giant insect among the plants. Michael's offspring playfully points a spray can at the dead Don and mows him down, in a shuddering reminder of machine guns and future generations of interchangeable godfathers and godsons.

Even before *The Godfather's* tremendous success Brando must have known he could only top it with a radical change of pace. He was briefly involved in Sidney Lumet's film version of *Child's Play*, but from the first rehearsal he must have realized that James Mason had the best role, was giving a superb performance, and would act anyone else off the screen. After Brando walked out, Robert Preston took his thankless part in what turned out to be a very disappointing film.

The real challenge for Brando came when Bernardo Bertolucci, the young Italian director of *Before the Revolution* and *The Conformist*, came to Brando with the bare elements of *Last Tango in Paris*. After hearing the story only once Brando agreed to do the film without even asking to read a finished screenplay. In his special, intuitive way he knew he would become the

script, the movie itself.

Bertolucci's film is a perversely romantic, almost psychotic valentine. Brando plays Paul, an American expatriate whose wife has just committed suicide. Crazed with grief, he roams the streets in Paris until, while apartment hunting, he faces an unknown girl across an empty room. "Death—the opposite is desire," Blanche DuBois once said, and Paul—a demented Kowalski—applies this credo, reaffirming his life force through orgasm. Brutally, without a word, he rapes the soon-compliant stranger. It should have been hit-and-run sex, but Paul stays at the scene of the erotic accident. Typical Brando character that he is, Paul decides to invent pure love out of pure sex.

While arranging his wife's funeral, Paul leases the apartment where he is to meet the puzzled girl for three frenzied afternoons. "No names here," he brusquely tells her, setting up the rules of the game. They are to shut out the world outside, forfeit their pasts and their identities, in a perilous experiment to know each other biblically but not well. Paul degrades the mesmerized Jeanne in every possible way, leveling all her inhibitions into sheer animality.

Like Blanche and Stella, Jeanne gets to know what it means "to get

LAST TANGO IN PARIS (1973). As Paul.

the colored lights going," and so does the audience, for with landmark audacity *Last Tango* dispenses with every hallowed film euphemism of crashing waves or bursting rockets to explore the ultimate mystery of body contact. Jeanne finds Paul's treatment so shockingly original that she even believes herself to be in love with the man who debases her—when she is only fascinated by her own capacity for debasement.

For Brando's Paul it is again a con game in reverse. He thinks he is using the girl, when she is really using him. Paul is soon dissatisfied with mere possession of her body; he must also have her mind. When she rejects his mad love to enter a comfortable marriage with her dull fiancé, Paul finally confesses: "I love you, you dummy." But the dummy has a corrupted little psyche of its own: she could stand physical but not mental rape. Twenty-odd years younger, the modern, callow Jeanne cannot face Paul's old-fashioned passion.

"I want to know your name," Paul whispers in the tenderest, most oblique revelation of his spiritual hunger. They are to be his last words, for the panicked girl shoots him at that very moment, with complete impunity. They are totally unconnected and she can tell the police a madman followed her and tried to rape her and that she killed him in self-defense. In a way this is exactly what has happened during their three days together. After all, she keeps repeating like an incantation that breaks the spell, "I never knew his name."

What Brando brings to *Last Tango in Paris* is something without precedent in his career. Into his other films he had put his talent; into this one he has put himself. Bertolucci's method is improvisational, and he has often said that he doesn't want actors to transform themselves into the characters but the other way around. After talking to Brando for ten minutes, he told Mel Gussow of *The New York Times*, he lost interest in Paul and became interested in Brando, instructing him to forget the part and remember what was inside him.

"He was hunting for all the secrets he had hidden in all his films," the director told Howard Kissel of *Woman's Wear Daily*. "He loved and hated improvising his scenes. He loved it because it was new for him and hated it because it seemed a violation of his privacy." As Brando works from within, several scenes in *Last Tango in Paris* transcend art and almost turn into psychodrama.

Paul welds Brando the man and Brando the actor; it is often painful to watch the seams. Like Terry Malloy, Paul is an ex-boxer; he played the bongos like young Buddy Brando. He was a revolutionary like Zapata, and he pursued the ideal of woman "through Africa, Asia and Indonesia." Then, in a monologue that transmutes personal embarrassment into powerful acting, Paul unburdens his load of bad memories as he muses: "My father was a drunk, a bar-brawler, very masculine. My mother was very poetic . . . and also a drunk." On and on he goes, through demonic versions of the sunny childhood anecdotes Brando had told inquisitive reporters through the years. Even his often quoted pleasure in milking the family cow in Evanston now evolves into a horror story of punishment and humiliation. Then he cuts the flow of words with a sharp laugh and says: "Maybe it's not true . . . maybe."

"Brando acted as my analyst and vice versa," Bertolucci told *The New York Times*. "I thought of him almost as a co-author." Indeed it is Brando's performance that rescues a baroque and distressingly uneven film. Only Brando has the equilibrium to walk Bertolucci's tightrope between the ridiculous and the sublime. Young Maria Schneider, obviously inspired by her co-star, is a credible partner. But how far *Tango* could have stumbled without Brando is evident whenever he is off-camera and the writer-director allows subplots to stagnate in self-indulgence, especially in the

LAST TANGO IN PARIS (1973).
With Maria Schneider.

LAST TANGO IN PARIS (1973). With Maria Schneider.

character of the girl's fiancé, not presented as a logically contrasting bourgeois type but as an addled *cinema verité* filmmaker. In scene after pointless scene Bertolucci coaxes the singularly maladroit Jean Pierre Léaud into making a fool of himself.

It is Brando's tragic dignity that permeates the film and carries it beyond morbid sentimentality and also beyond pornography. The intimacy between Paul and Jeanne is as lacking in real pleasure as a clinical operation or a psychiatric confessional. It is not eroticism but exorcism of private demons. Between one meaningless contact and the next Paul remembers Rosa, his dead wife, and weeps in a corner of the room. Then, in a beautifully sustained monologue, he berates Rosa's body, still lying in its bier, showering her with every possible insult until he breaks into loving sobs, asking her the one impossible question: "Who the hell were you?"

This impossibility of really knowing anyone is *Tango's* inner rhythm. "Hell is other people," a Sartre character said, and Bertolucci's undeniable sense of color and decor converts the apartment building in which the lovers meet into a visual metaphor of hell, complete with a crazy attendant who laughingly dispenses keys to rooms with no spiritual exit. In their bare, round, closed chambe[r] Paul explores the otherness o[f] Jeanne, constantly stifling a huma[n] necessity for something beyon[d] mere physical coupling.

His system fails. Just as he los[es] Rosa by trying to know her to[o] well, he loses the young strange[r] by choosing to know her too little[.] As Jeanne eludes him, Paul'[s] anguish becomes intolerable, in [the] last half hour where Brando carrie[s] the film wildly, recklessly. "It i[s] finished," Jeanne insists, but Pau[l] will not let her go. They argue in [a] dance hall where a tango contest i[s] in progress; the dancers movin[g] around them like elegant wind-u[p] dolls, in contrast with Paul's raw suffering. Before an astonished now frightened Jeanne, he goe[s] into a self-destructive orgy as h[e] crouches, kneels, strips, and drun[k]enly rolls on the floor. "It's love,["] he shouts at the angry proprietres[s] who wants him out of the cabaret[.] "It's a contest," she answers[.] "Where does love fit in?"

For Paul and Jeanne, no matte[r] how hard he has tried, it has als[o] been a contest where love coul[d] never fit in. Their grappling an[d] wrestling was merely another bou[t] in the battle of the sexes, a cliché the film brings into new, disturbing life. About to lose the girl irrevoca[b]ly, Paul breaks the no-name pac[t] by suddenly calling her Rosa, unconsciously pronouncing he[r] dead, just like his wife.

The last scene climaxes the integration of Paul and Brando, creature and creator. Right after the girl shoots him, he staggers to the balcony and—in a masterful touch—takes out a wad of chewing gum from his mouth and presses it against the railing: the last spilling of his inner being, of his guts. "There's nothing more to give," his blurry eyes seem to be saying as he looks straight at the audience, silently pleading for final release. According to Bertolucci, when the shooting was over, Brando said: "I will never do something like that again. That's the last time I use up my energies."

In the context of Brando's career the film's conclusion is simultaneously exhilarating and sad. Here is a man at the point of achieving a form of greatness that leaves him ultimately unsatisfied. Soon after, he was telling *Oui* magazine: "In a funny way, I never was an actor. I suppose I never really knew what I wanted to do or what was possible for me to do. I acted because I was trained to do nothing else to make a living, but now I think it's coming to an end."

Once again Brando insists he will retire to his island in Tahiti, with a group of superior, intellectual human beings who will use *The Whole Earth Catalogue* as a mod-

ern bible for survival, to rebuild paradise on earth in an unpolluted utopia, run on solar energy and chicken manure. He may keep his promise this time, or he may come back and star in twenty more films. No one can tell, for this man's life repeats itself in cycles—same tune, different orchestration—like Ravel's *Bolero*. One way or another, it doesn't really matter; he has left too much of himself behind. Projectors are as merciless as life; it is too late for Brando to turn either into reverse motion.

Primitive people refuse to be photographed, in fear that a part of their soul, a fragment of their virtue, will be lost in every image. For more than two decades Marlon Brando has given his truth away, 24 times a second. It is there, stubborn and unstoppable, in light and shadow. The images he created are public property, forever. They rise again, at the flick of a switch, at the click of a sprocket.

He gave us Malloy and Wilocek, Penderton and Walker, Corleone and Paul. They are our treasured gifts from a great actor. And in the irretrievable art of film no one—not even Marlon Brando—can erase the past. Whether he regrets the world he gained is his own personal problem. But the screen will eternally profit from having once possessed his soul.

145

POSTSCRIPT

On March 27, 1973, almost eighteen years to the date from his delighted acceptance of his first Oscar, Marlon Brando was again selected best actor of the year for *The Godfather*. He did not reply to the invitation to the ceremony and everyone felt he would more or less follow the path of recent winners of Academy Awards, who were either reluctant or rebellious.

George C. Scott had ignored the honor altogether. Jane Fonda had received it with a curt and eloquent "I have a lot to say but..." For Brando, this was clearly not enough. He dreamed up something far more spectacular and as his name was announced, a stunned Liv Ullmann was confronted onstage by an Apache maiden in full tribal dress, who rejected the statuette with shaking head and waving hand.

Sacheen Littlefeather then explained that Brando's position on behalf of oppressed American Indians precluded his acceptance of the award from an industry that had so crudely insulted Indians over the years. Followed by a mixture of applause and booing, Miss Little feather left the stage with Brando' statement unread: acceptance speeches were limited to one min ute and the text of Brando's rejec tion—as later published in *The New York Times*—could easily have rambled on for ten.

Later opinion about Brando' coup were as divided as the jeer and cheers that split that night' audience at Los Angeles' Chandle Pavilion. Some felt that Brando' point was weakened by his lack o courage to defend it and by hi sending Miss Littlefeather to fac the audience in his place. Man argued that a resident of Wounde Knee would have been a more con vincing exponent of ethnic griev ances against Hollywood than Mis Littlefeather, a veteran of the tele vision serial *Dark Shadows* an winner of a studio contest as Mis Vampire of 1972.

Undoubtedly Brando narrowe the scope of his cause by hinging i on Hollywood misrepresentation o Indians, a quite belated claim afte decades of films—from *Broker Lance* and *Apache* to *Little Bi*

Man and *Soldier Blue*—in which ndians were heroic victims of reacherous Whites. Inevitably, he Italo-American Anti-Defamation League quickly seized the occasion to chide Brando for making a stand for the Indians while winning an Oscar for a film portrait hey considered highly offensive.

The Hollywood contingent, of course, was infuriated. On stage to announce the Best Actress award, Raquel Welch sourly quipped: "I hope the winner doesn't have a cause." Clint Eastwood, before naming *The Godfather* as Best Film, wondered about giving equal ime to all the cowboys killed in John Ford Westerns. It was mild criticism compared to the industry's reaction to what they generally considered a stunt.

The Hollywood Reporter headlined: "Brando Caper Called Gutless, Tasteless" and quoted Academy official Charlton Heston as saying: "It was childish. The American Indian needs better friends than that." While Michael Caine—one of Brando's four rivals for the award—declared: "I agree entirely with what he did, but he should have stood up and done it himself instead of letting the girl get the boos. I think a man who makes two million dollars playing the leader of the Mafia would at least give half of it to the Indians." And just like twenty years before, when the Kowalski take-off was a night club comedian's staple, many tiresome jokes started doing the rounds about Brando, the Indian giver.

All in all, few doubted Brando's sincerity. It was the method that was deplored by friend and foe alike. For the Oscar, refused or not, remains his for the record. On the final count, Brando managed to have his cake and eat it. His gesture on Oscar night was at best another in a series of empty ones. And at worst the last—or latest—of his anti-Hollywood pranks. In the same childish way he had toyed with his first Oscar, he had petulantly rejected the second.

And so, Marlon Brando was still fanning the flames of his eternal love-hate relationship with the movies, with his audience, with himself. Once again he was paid in kind with an equal love-hate polarization. "We've had enough of him, this is the end of Brando," millions were snorting as they switched off their TV sets on that Oscar night. And yet, looking back on his career, the incident was a quality of *deja vu* as one more of the endless cliffhangers in a movie life Brando has chosen to live in serial fashion. The only safe way to conclude the present installment is by prudently flashing the ever-handy, non-committal title card: "To be continued..."

BIBLIOGRAPHY

Alpert, Hollis, *The Dream and the Dreamers*, New York: The Macmillan Company, 1962

Baxter, John, *Hollywood in the Sixties*, New York: A. S. Barnes & Co., 1972

Brian, Denis, *Tallulah, Darling*, New York: Pyramid Publications, 1972

Capote, Truman, *The Duke in His Domain*, New York: Random House, 1962

Clurman, Harold, *On Directing*, New York: The Macmillan Company, 1972

Durgnat, Raymond, *Films and Feelings*, Cambridge, Mass.: M.I.T. Press, 1971

Easty, Edward D., *On Method Acting*, New York: HC Publishers, 1966

Graham, Sheilah, *Confessions of a Hollywood Columnist*, New York: William Morrow & Co., 1969

Houston, Penelope, *The Contemporary Cinema*, Baltimore: Penguin Books, 1963

Houseman, John, *Run-Through*, New York: Simon and Schuster, 1972

Kael, Pauline, *Kiss Kiss Bang Bang*, Boston: Little, Brown & Co., 1968

Kauffman, Stanley, *A World of Film*, New York: Harper & Row, 1966

Morella, Joe and Edward Z. Epstein, *Rebels*, Secaucus: The Citadel Press, 1971

Morin, Edgar, *The Stars*, New York: Grove Press, 1961

Parsons, Louella, *Tell it to Louella*, New York: G. P. Putnam's Sons, 1961

Puzo, Mario, *The Godfather Papers*, New York: G.P. Putnam's Sons, 1972

Ross, Lillian and Helen, *The Player*, New York: Simon and Schuster, 1962

Schickel, Richard, *The Stars*, New York: The Dial Press, 1962

Schumach, Murray, *The Face on the Cutting Room Floor*, New York: William Morrow & Co., 1964

Shipman, David, *The Great Movie Stars: The International Years*, New York: St. Martin's Press, 1973

Simon, John, *Private Screenings*, New York: The Macmillan Company, 1967

Steen, Mike, *A Look at Tennessee Williams*, New York: Hawthorn Books, 1969

Walker, Alexander, *Stardom*, New York: Stein & Day, 1970

Wood, Robin, *Arthur Penn*, New York: Praeger, 1970

THE FILMS OF MARLON BRANDO

*The director's name follows the release date. A (c) following the release date indicates
that the film was in color. Sp indicates screenplay and b/o indicates based/on.*

1. THE MEN, United Artists, 1950, *Fred Zinnemann*, Sp: Carl Foreman.
Cast: Teresa Wright, Everett Sloane, Jack Webb. Brando is a paraplegic
war veteran rebelling against his fate and then accepting it.

2. A STREETCAR NAMED DESIRE, Warner Brothers, 1951, *Elia Kazan*,
Sp: Tennessee Williams, adapted from his play by Oscar Saul. Cast: Vivien
Leigh, Kim Hunter, Karl Malden. Brando is the brutish laborer in conflict
with his delicate sister-in-law.

3. VIVA ZAPATA!, 20th Century-Fox, 1952, *Elia Kazan*, Sp: John Steinbeck
b/o the novel *Zapata the Unconquerable* by Edgcumb Pinchon. Cast: Jean
Peters, Anthony Quinn, Joseph Wiseman, Mildred Dunnock, Margo.
Brando as the Mexican revolutionary.

4. JULIUS CAESAR, MGM, 1953, *Joseph L. Mankiewicz*, Sp: Joseph L.
Mankiewicz b/o play by Shakespeare. Cast: James Mason, John Gielgud,
Louis Calhern, Edmond O'Brien, Greer Garson, Deborah Kerr. Brando as
Marc Antony, avenger of Caesar's death.

5. THE WILD ONE, Columbia, 1954, *Laslo Benedek*, Sp: John Paxton, b/o
story by Frank Rooney. Cast: Mary Murphy, Robert Keith, Lee Marvin,
Jay C. Flippen. Brando is the leader of a gang of motorcyclist-hoodlums
invading a small town.

6. ON THE WATERFRONT, Columbia, 1954, *Elia Kazan*, Sp: Budd Schulberg, b/o story by Schulberg and articles by Malcolm Johnson. Cast: Eva
Marie Saint, Karl Malden, Lee J. Cobb, Rod Steiger. Brando received an
Academy Award for his performance as a dock laborer rebelling against
mob control of unions.

7. DESIREE, 20th Century-Fox, 1954, (c), *Henry Koster*, Sp: Daniel Taradash, b/o novel by Annemarie Selinko. Cast: Jean Simmons, Merle Oberon, Michael Rennie, Cameron Mitchell. Brando as Napoleon in love and war.

8. GUYS AND DOLLS, MGM, 1955, (c), *Joseph L. Mankiewicz*, Sp: Joseph L. Mankiewicz, b/o the musical by Jo Swerling and Abe Burrows. Cast: Jean Simmons, Frank Sinatra, Vivian Blaine. Brando is a gambler who bets he can seduce a "Salvation Army doll."

9. THE TEAHOUSE OF THE AUGUST MOON, MGM, 1956, (c), *Daniel Mann*, Sp: John Patrick, b/o his play and the book by Vern J. Schneider. Cast: Glenn Ford, Machiko Kyo, Paul Ford, Eddie Albert. Brando is an Okinawan interpreter who fools the U.S. Army.

10. SAYONARA, Warner Brothers, 1957, (c), *Joshua Logan*, Sp: Paul Osborn, b/o novel by James Michener. Cast: Miiko Taka, Red Buttons, Miyoshi Umeki, Kent Smith. Brando is an Air Force hero who jeopardizes his career by falling in love with a Japanese girl.

11. THE YOUNG LIONS, 20th Century-Fox, 1958, *Edward Dmytryk*, Sp: Edward Anhalt, b/o novel by Irwin Shaw. Cast: Montgomery Clift, Dean Martin, Maximilian Schell, Hope Lange, May Britt. Brando as a disillusioned Nazi officer.

12. THE FUGITIVE KIND, United Artists, 1960, *Sidney Lumet*, Sp: Tennessee Williams and Meade Roberts, b/o Williams's play *Orpheus Descending*. Cast: Anna Magnani, Joanne Woodward, Maureen Stapleton, Victor Jory. Brando as a modern Orpheus pursued by small-town furies.

13. ONE-EYED JACKS, Paramount, 1961, (c), *Marlon Brando*, Sp: Guy Trosper and Calder Willingham, b/o novel *The Authentic Death of Hendry Jones* by Charles Neider. Cast: Karl Malden, Katy Jurado, Ben Johnson, Pina Pellicer. Brando directs himself as a betrayed bandit seeking revenge.

14. MUTINY ON THE BOUNTY, MGM, 1962, (c), *Lewis Milestone*, Sp: Charles Lederer, b/o novel by Charles Nordhoff and James Norman Hall. Cast: Trevor Howard, Richard Harris, Hugh Griffith, Tarita. Brando as the first mate who challenges despotic Captain Bligh. Remake of the 1935 film, with Brando in the Clark Gable role.

15. THE UGLY AMERICAN, Universal, 1963, (c), *George Englund*, Sp: Stewart Stern, b/o book by Eugene Burdick and William J. Lederer. Cast: Eiji Okada, Sandra Church, Arthur Hill, Pat Hingle. Brando as the U.S. ambassador to a mythical Southeast Asian country on the brink of civil war.

16. BEDTIME STORY, Universal, 1964, (c), *Ralph Levy*, Sp: Stanley Shapiro and Paul Henning. Cast: David Niven, Shirley Jones, Dody Goodman, Marie Windsor. Brando is the con man who seduces and fleeces women.

17. THE SABOTEUR: CODE NAME MORITURI, 20th Century-Fox, 1965, *Bernhard Wicki*, Sp: Daniel Taradash, b/o novel *Morituri* by Werner Joerg Luedecke. Cast: Yul Brynner, Trevor Howard, Janet Margolin. Brando as an anti-Nazi German commissioned to sabotage a cargo ship.

18. THE CHASE, Columbia, 1966, (c), *Arthur Penn*, Sp: Lillian Hellman, b/o novel and play by Horton Foote. Cast: Jane Fonda, Robert Redford, E. G. Marshall, Angie Dickinson, Miriam Hopkins, James Fox, Robert Duvall, Janice Rule. Brando as a sheriff trying to bring law and order to a town in uproar.

19. THE APPALOOSA, Universal, 1966, (c), *Sidney J. Furie*, Sp: James Bridges and Roland Kibbee, b/o novel by Robert MacLeod. Cast: John Saxon, Anjanette Comer, Emilio Fernández. Brando as a would-be rancher trying to recover a stolen horse.

20. A COUNTESS FROM HONG KONG, Universal, 1967, (c), *Charles Chaplin*, Sp: Charles Chaplin. Cast: Sophia Loren, Sydney Chaplin, Tippi Hedren, Margaret Rutherford. Shipboard farce about an ambassador who finds a stowaway countess in his cabin.

21. REFLECTIONS IN A GOLDEN EYE, Warner Brothers, 1967, (c), *John Huston*, Sp: Gladys Hill and Chapman Mortimer, b/o novel by Carson McCullers. Cast: Elizabeth Taylor, Julie Harris, Brian Keith, Robert Forster. Brando as a homosexual major in a Southern Army post.

22. THE NIGHT OF THE FOLLOWING DAY, Universal, 1968, (c), *Hubert Cornfield*, Sp: Hubert Cornfield and Robert Phippeny, b/o novel *The Snatchers* by Lionel White. Cast: Richard Boone, Pamela Franklin, Rita Moreno, Jess Hahn. Brando is the chauffeur-kidnapper in a young heiress' nightmare.

23. CANDY, MGM, 1968, (c), *Christian Marquand*, Sp: Buck Henry, b/o novel by Terry Southern and Mason Hoffenberg. Cast: Ewa Aulin, Richard Burton, James Coburn, Walter Matthau, John Huston, Charles Aznavour, Ringo Starr. Brando in a sketch as a libidinous Guru.

24. BURN!, United Artists, 1970, (c), *Gillo Pontecorvo*, Sp: Franco Solinas and Giorgio Arlorio. Cast: Evaristo Márquez, Renato Salvatori. Brando is the British *agent provocateur* who aids and abets revolution in a Portuguese colony.

25. THE NIGHTCOMERS, Avco Embassy, 1972, (c), *Michael Winner,* Sp: Michael Hastings, b/o characters from *The Turn of the Screw* by Henry James. Cast: Stephanie Beacham, Harry Andrews, Thora Hird, Verna Harvey, Christopher Ellis. Brando is the gardener who enthralls the children of the manor into innocent murder.

26. THE GODFATHER, Paramount, 1972, (c), *Francis Ford Coppola,* Sp: Mario Puzo and Francis Ford Coppola, b/o novel by Puzo. Cast: Al Pacino, James Caan, Robert Duvall, Richard Castellano, Richard Conte, Sterling Hayden, Diane Keaton. Brando as the aging Mafia chief reluctantly drawn into gang warfare. For this film he won and rejected his second Oscar.

27. LAST TANGO IN PARIS, United Artists, 1973, (c), *Bernardo* Bertolucci, Sp: Bernardo Bertolucci and Franco Arcalli. Cast: Maria Schneider, Jean-Pierre Léaud. Brando as a widower erotically involved with a young girl on the verge of marrying another man.

INDEX

(Page numbers italicized indicate photographs)

154

156

Sturges, John   94

ABOUT THE AUTHOR

René Jordan has written extensively on films for many publications, including
Film Quarterly, *The Village Voice*, *Films in Review*, *Cinema*, and *Film
Ideal*. He is the author of *Clark Gable*, a Pyramid Illustrated History of the
Movies. He lives in New York City.

ABOUT THE EDITOR

Ted Sennett has been attending and enjoying movies since the age of two. He
has written about films for magazines and newspapers, and is the author of
Warner Brothers Presents, a survey of the great Warners films of the thirties and forties. A publishing executive, he lives in New Jersey with his
wife and three children.